DEEP THOUGHTS FROM THE SHALLOW END

ALAN HOFFLER

WRITE ANGLE PUBLISHING

Deep Thoughts from the Shallow End

Printed in the United States of America
ISBN 979-8-9922314-0-3

Book layout by CSinclaire Write-Design LLC
Cover design by Allyson Hoffler

WRITE ANGLE
PUBLISHING

Other Books by Alan Hoffler

Presentation Sin: The Practical Guide to Stop Offending (and Start Impressing) Your Audience

6 Steps Forward: Every Man Matters

Silver Goldfish: Loud & Clear: The 10 Keys to Delivering Memorable Business Presentations

Acknowledgment and Thanks

While there are many people who have contributed unknowingly to my life and thoughts, there are specific people who should be called out.

- Dad: Your vocabulary makes anyone think more deeply. Your character and commitment to what you've thought are great examples for the many you've touched. I laugh when I think of your quote, given a few weeks before the manuscript was finalized: "These are my thoughts, and I think that I'm right." Yep.
- Friday morning men's group: We've solved the world's problems, many times over. I'm grateful for the outlet.
- The mentees who have dared walk with me: your questions and challenges made me a better man.
- The Fellas: From those original "pizza and tears" nights to the mountain hikes and wilderness adventures to our annual beach extravaganza, the conversations and challenge to think deeper have been a staple of our enduring friendships.
- Derek Blacksher: It's rare to find someone so committed, so driven, and so fun. You were the perfect complement to my dreams for this stage of life. Your hunger and love for metaphors makes me think more deeply.

Contents

Ooh, That's Deep 1
Anyone Can Produce Deep Thoughts. 7
Setting 15
Organizing Deep Thoughts 18
Relationships and People 21
Habits & Behavior 44
Time. 65
Work & Money 77
Stuff 88
Death 101
Legacy 109
Mind & Emotions 125
World Problems 134
God 154
The Beach 167
Near-death Experiences 179
Questions (Without Answers) 195
So What? 198
About the Author. 203
Future Books by Alan Hoffler. 205

The purpose in a man's heart is like deep water,
but a man of understanding will draw it out.

Proverbs 20:5 (ESV)

1

Ooh, That's Deep

As a lifelong teacher, creating and assimilating content is a way of life. I've functioned as a math instructor, corporate trainer, keynote speaker, Sunday School teacher, business owner, mentor, and friend. I've taught lessons ranging from integration by parts to time management to the Sermon on the Mount. In every case, there are people who are smarter and more qualified to teach than I am. Knowing that, I ~~steal~~ repurpose content from a variety of sources on a regular basis.

When I listen to a message, read a book, watch a TEDx video, or take a class, my first thought is usually, "Oh, that would be better if . . ." or "I could use that in my talk on . . . ." I've joked—and it may be true—that I've only ever had two original thoughts in my life.

As I've listened to inspirational speakers, dynamic teachers, compelling leaders, and subject matter experts, I always felt . . . insignificant. Inferior. An imposter as a teacher. They know things I don't know. They think ways I don't think.

They write things I can't write. They say things in ways I can't—or don't—say them.

My head spins as I listen to and read philosophers and apologists and scientists and pundits of the day wax eloquently and give opinions and predictions. Often, I agree with them. Whether I agree because of their compelling communication or I had a conviction in alignment with them is hard to ascertain. I'm faced with the realization that there are a lot of topics I haven't given much thought to. One idea seems as good to me as another. And that bothers me. I want to be more well-read. I want to know more and have more clarity around the issues that affect me and be conversant in all the rest.

I'll hear a phrase given in rhythm and rhyme and think, Why didn't I think of that? I read books and have "This is amazing! How utterly simple and transforming!" moments, but when faced with a blank piece of paper or an open document, I too often have felt powerless to create.

Oh, I had plenty of people give me accolades and compliments for my teaching and insight. You can make a splash and even sound smart using other people's content. But I always felt that I was nothing but an imposter improver. I could take something someone else did or said and make it better. But an original and deep thinker? That wasn't who I thought I was.

When I interact with and see behind the curtains of speakers and teachers I admire, one thing always stands out: they are massive consumers of content. They read. They show clear evidence of being quiet and spending time thinking. Maybe they limit their thinking to one area of expertise. I don't know the breadth of their thinking; only that they show depth in what I hear them say.

But who has the time to consume, to watch, to read, to listen? Many of my friends ask or urge me to watch syndicated TV or streaming series. I can't even get my work done and spend time with my family, much less watch entertainment for several hours a night. And if I do have time to consume material, while mindless entertainment has an appeal and likely a dopamine rush, I feel like I should be listening, learning, leading.

A friend of mine who is a business and life coach told me one of his wealthy clients said to him, "I want you to tell me what you've learned every week. I don't have time to read and watch videos. I'm going to count on you to find interesting things to share with me." Seems unfair . . . being rich enough to afford to have someone else read, listen, and think for you. But as I dug a little deeper into my favorite authors and speakers, most of them are recycling, reusing, and repurposing.

Dan and Chip Heath, one of my favorite author duos, are both professors at prestigious universities. They have graduate students and foundations doing research and compiling examples for their excellent books. Stan Phelps, the co-author of my second book *Silver Goldfish*, wrote his first book (*Purple Goldfish*) by crowd-sourcing a thousand examples of companies doing more than the expected (lagniappe). He took those examples, categorized them, and now speaks all over the world as an expert on customer experience (among other things). I heard Jim Collins (author of the classic *Good to Great*) talk at a conference. He had a think tank devoted to studying businesses and what made them great. His name is on the cover; the data and facts and conclusions came from a lot of others.

I don't disparage these authors and leaders for having others do the heavy lifting on developing their content. I admire and, in some cases, nearly worship them. But their processes and their methods are worth studying almost as much as their conclusions.

It was during one of my moments of awe at someone's eloquent point that I heard myself think or say—it's hard to tell the difference in my world since I process things verbally—"Ooh, that's deep." And the normal thoughts of inferiority quickly followed as I also thought, "I wish I could come up with Deep Thoughts like that."

I felt like I was shallow compared to the deep thinkers I heard. And that's how the title for this work was born. Somewhere along the way, I found the process to help me have Deep Thoughts like the people I admired. Eventually, I came to believe that I was a Deep Thinker with something to share.

We're a few pages in. It's probably time to define what I mean by a Deep Thought. The very acknowledgment of the term implies that not all thoughts are created equal. Some thoughts are obvious and instant. Others fleeting and not remembered. Some are ridiculous and should be forgotten. Many thoughts aren't true or healthy, but cannot be forgotten. What, then, is a Deep Thought?

I have three aspects that define a Deep Thought and give hope to those of us aspiring to become deep thinkers. First, a Deep Thought must be pondered anew. It isn't what you've always thought. It isn't the first reaction. It isn't the obvious conclusion. It takes some amount of effort to consider.

"I love pizza." Not deep.

"Who wears striped pants with a plaid shirt?" Not deep.

"It's more humid today than yesterday." Not deep.

I find that prompts from others help this thinking process immensely. A good question can spawn a pool full of Deep Thoughts. Back-and-forth between thinkers is healthy.

Here's a not so Deep Thought but a pertinent observation: thoughts are inside us. You can't know what I'm thinking unless I tell you. We've all heard people say, "I know what you're thinking . . . ," but that statement can't possibly be true all the time. You might be right, but you're just as likely to be wrong, especially if I'm in Deep Thought.

This leaves us with another marker to define a Deep Thought. Deep Thoughts are shared and cause other people to think Deep Thoughts. You can't know my thoughts if I don't share them.

I share lots of thoughts that aren't deep. The difference is in what the thought does to and for the listener. If you can't remember what I said, it wasn't a very Deep Thought. If you're daydreaming about what you'll do this afternoon, I'm not expressing a Deep Thought. Deep Thoughts connect. They demand thought from the listener. The listener may not agree. They may have a different Deep Thought. But if you can cause someone else to think, then we'll call it a Deep Thought.

In my work as a public speaking coach, I deal daily with people who are scared to speak up. It's hard to know if their issue is the mechanics of speaking or the inferiority complex of sharing what they're thinking. Regardless, they are hindered from sharing whatever is on their mind. And that's a shame. Society is less for their reticence.

Publishing a book is risky. It's quite likely that not everyone will love this work. I am quite sure that I've not thought through everything I write and there are holes in my logic and inefficiency in my delivery (although I'm counting on my very capable editor to minimize the latter). I doubt over time that the book will receive all five-star reviews. And yet, there is profit in sharing. If your response is, "This is garbage," but you're thinking later about why it's garbage, then I've accomplished exactly what a Deep Thinker hopes.

In summary, Deep Thoughts are:

- outside the realm of normal thoughts. They are revisited and vetted and make you (thinker or hearer) realize something new.

- thoughts that must be remembered.

- shared with others and cause them to think.

2

Anyone Can Produce Deep Thoughts

I'm not dumber than the people I admired. I don't have less time, potential, or ambition than they do. Well, maybe less ambition. But after more than twenty years on stage, I began to warm up to the idea that I had something to say. I had to embrace the title of "expert" even though I didn't feel like one. A colleague once told me that people pay to hear experts. If I want my training consultancy to be successful, I need to be seen as an expert. It doesn't matter how I feel.

Because I'm now an author of a book about Deep Thoughts and I've discovered that I've had at least one original thought and a few that have had an impact on others, I'll declare myself an expert on Deep Thinking and give you a roadmap forward to have Deep Thoughts yourself.

Deep Thoughts don't automatically come charging from the abyss if you spend time in meditation. They aren't spawned by burning incense, assuming a particular physical position, or reciting incantations. They can't be scheduled. They just appear. While they can show up at any time and at any place, they seem to come most often through a predictable system. Here are three elements that can lead you to having more and better Deep Thoughts.

First, Deep Thoughts are a subset of thoughts. If you have more thoughts—even shallow thoughts—you'll increase the chances that you'll have Deep Thoughts. But it starts with thinking. This is a problem for most people in the modern Western world. We don't take time to think. We're too busy doing and visiting and traveling and watching and going and browsing and feeling and posting and complaining. Perhaps the greatest thing about the ancient world was that activity stopped when the sun set, and people had time to think.

Taking (making) time to think is difficult. It doesn't matter where or when you take the time to think. I personally love sunrises and sunsets, especially if they're over a body of water. If I travel to the beach, I will wake up early to watch the sunrise and arrange my schedule to be at water's edge at sunset.

I also love the lawnmower for thinking. I am blessed with a couple of acres that require my attention every couple of weeks. People have told me I'm old enough and rich enough that I should hire some neighbor kid to mow for me. They don't understand: that's thinking time for me. Sacred time.

I have a regular spot at the lake I enjoy. I climb on my Perception Pilot pedal kayak and spend an hour on the calm water, thinking. When I travel, I'll ask the hotel clerk where the best place in town is to watch the sunset. If I can't have one of those special thinking spots to enjoy, then every morning I'm at home, right after breakfast, I retire to a chair in my living room next to a window, pull out a journal, and spend time reading, reflecting, and thinking.

Sadly, none of those practices were a regular part of my life a few years back. Yes, I am more financially well off, have gotten my kids out of the house, and have a greater command of my schedule than I did a decade or two ago. Those factors contribute to my ability to schedule thinking time. But anyone can find the time if they make it a priority. Thinking time is precious time. Deep Thinkers find time to think. And thinking is best done without earbuds and podcasts. Silence is the best soundtrack for Deep Thinkers.

The second key aspect of Deep Thoughts is that they must be remembered. I've had a dozen million-dollar ideas in my life that I later cannot recall. I know they were great, but they disappeared. I've written books and movies and solved the world's problems several times over in my mind, but I never captured the details to remember them for later. It is appalling how much I forget.[1] I do not trust my mind to remember, so I need a tool to help me.

One pastor I admire let it be known that he always carries a black notebook with him where he writes down observations, thoughts, and quotes. I've heard him speak many times, and he often allows Q&A in his talks. Inevitably, someone will ask, "What is the latest entry in your black book?" He'll pull it out from his jacket and read a few lines. What impresses me each time is not the presence of a black analog notebook. It's that he has current entries. They weren't notes from seminary decades ago. They were not the thoughts from his meditation retreat last month. They weren't what he consumed at the staff meeting last

1 One of my favorite examples is Hermann Ebbinghaus' *Forgetting Curve*. His "science" was horrid. His conclusion was spot on: humans forget a lot. Look him up on Wikipedia.

week. They were what he had seen or heard that day. And they always seemed deep. At least to me.

I've never been known for discipline. I've lost at least 50 pounds in every year of my adult life. But I gain an average of 51 pounds each year as well. I've started gardens, woodworking projects, hobbies, and friendships that have all faltered in flaming failure due to my lack of attention and follow-through. How could I possibly find a way to keep and catalog all the material and thoughts I consume in a given week, day, or hour?

The answer came in the form of technology, which I have a tenuous relationship with. I started trying to capture notes digitally in 2010. I eventually settled on the Microsoft product OneNote, distributed with their Office suite. It's available on my computer, my phone, my tablet, and online. It can absorb my input offline, like on a plane or on a camping trip on the side of a mountain, and then sync that content when I return to "civilization." It seems to handle large amounts of data easily. I can forward an email to it with the click of a button and take pictures with my phone and have them on the cloud and indexed in seconds. I can add audio recordings, process hyperlinks to web pages, tag articles, and even draw. It can record my voice, so I can read a book and talk to OneNote as I hit passages I'd like to capture. Those spoken words magically appear in my notes. In short, OneNote captures and catalogs everything I can send it. It solves the problem of capturing my thoughts and observations.

It helps to have those entries organized. I have a notebook for my business. One for my family. My hobbies. My writing. My non-profit work. Church. Recipes. And books. Each notebook has multiple sections. Each section can have a gazillion "pages" which is probably equivalent to a note. It's interesting—or maybe it shows how bad software developers are at understanding clients and naming features—that nowhere in OneNote can you actually create a "note." But once you learn how it works and create habits and a system that works for you, it's an indispensable tool. At least for me. I went all in on capturing everything in my life in OneNote by 2019.

By far, the most valuable feature of the tool is the "search" function. Assuming I spelled correctly, I can find notes I made a decade ago in mere seconds. Wonder what was said in a client conversation? Click. Search. Found. Need that recipe for hot pepper jelly? Nearly instantaneous. Want to know what the preacher said on Palm Sunday in 2019? No problem. Everything I've ever entered is searchable for me to find, quickly, from anywhere in the world.

You can use Evernote. Or Word. Or a Remarkable tablet. Or a piece of paper (although that's hardly searchable). Or a little black notebook. The key is to capture what you're consuming. Start yesterday. If you didn't, start today.

> The best time to plant a tree was twenty years ago.
> The second-best time is today.
> ***— Chinese proverb***

By the way, that quote shows up in three separate pages, in three separate contexts, in my OneNote archive. Here's one I hope you put in your archive, and your life:

> The best time to start logging your thoughts was twenty years ago. The second-best time is today.
> ***— Alan Hoffler, Deep Thinker***

In January of 2019, I started a note called "Ideas / Deep Thoughts." It was designed to collect quotes I could use in my weekly teaching at church. It quickly became a place for me to dump book reviews, quotes, web pages, and aphorisms. I began to refer to it as "Deep thoughts from the shallow end." It was a nod to the fact that I was consuming material from people I felt were deeper and more sophisticated thinkers than I was. I sat in the shallows while I admired their depth.

My goal was to have something current every week to share with my class. Some weeks I had a lot. I once taught a whole hour on nothing but the Deep Thoughts I had the previous week. Some weeks I had nothing to share. Perhaps I was too busy, or too depressed, or too self-centered to collect a Deep Thought.

One day I had a class member tell me, in all sincerity, "I've come to look forward to your Deep Thoughts more than your teaching." And he added, without too much of a pause, but also without much inflection, "Which is great, of course." I chose not to take offense.

The weird thing was, I agreed. I looked forward to sharing current, thought-provoking content much more than the organized and researched lesson I was commissioned to teach. As I consume and collect more material, that desire only increases.

Which leads to my secret sauce. Take notes about everything. When I wrote my first book, *Presentation Sin,* it started as a compilation of blog posts I had made, organized and edited by someone else in the style of prose (thanks, Karin!). Those blog posts were the result of hundreds of pages of notes about speakers I had taken in every context I found myself: funerals, conferences, meetings, movies, churches, political speeches, and private conversations. I took LOTS of notes. I wrote about them. And they became a book. Which makes me a published author. To some, that makes me an expert. I'm able to cash dozens of dollars a year from my royalties. And I give a copy of the book to anyone who seems remotely interested in hiring me to talk or teach about communication.

But that highlights our third and last component of Deep Thoughts. They need to be shared. Thoughts that stay in your own head can only affect you. But a shared thought can spark a revolution. I realized that all those people I admired and felt inferior to were doing one thing I wasn't: they were sharing their insights and thoughts about the world with the world. As I shared more, my influence grew and my depth increased. People shared back, bounced ideas off me, and thoughts went deeper still. Hiding in a cave (or home office) cataloging my own thoughts only fills my hard drive and is lost to history. Our insights were made to be shared with the world.

When I was reviewing my life purpose and goals several years ago, I came to the realization that the best way to have a legacy was to leave a permanent record of things I wanted to say. This was spawned by a Deep Thought via a podcast: "Twenty-five years after you die, no one is even going to be saying your name." To me, that meant I needed to be a writer. Not just a writer. After all, I had already published three books. But a prolific writer.

No one is going to comb through my OneNote cache after I'm gone. But they might read a book I wrote. I sat down and thought of all the books I could write that could encapsulate my thoughts on a variety of subjects. The list is constantly expanding, but I've come up with over 30 books I want to write. Most have titles; many already have outlines.[2] One of those books, under the heading "Life" in my Books to Write page in my Notes for Writing Section of my Writing notebook, is titled Deep Thoughts from the Shallow End. When I wrote the title, I probably only had a few dozen entries in my Deep Thoughts and Ideas page. Now I have almost four thousand words in that document (not quite a full book, but that's a good chunk of sentences and phrases to build on).

As I began writing them down in prose form, I ended up adding a lot of autobiographical elements as I reflected on events and lessons from my life. One of the definitions of maturity I like is "the ability to learn from other people's mistakes." Maybe this compilation will allow you to mature.

So here we are. If you're reading this, you are consuming several aspects of my life. It's a bucket list/life goal to publish these thoughts. It's a collection of thoughts and challenges on some of the issues and events that have shaped my life. It's a discipline I've created to deepen my own life and perspective. And it's my effort to share a thinking system that will help you gain clarity about and influence in the world in which you live.

But most of all, it's a challenge for you to think more deeply. I doubt you will agree with everything I've written. I hope you don't. But I want you to THINK. So many of our world's problems could be solved by critical thinking. That starts with me and with you. Think frequently and deeply, catalog your thoughts, and share them, no matter how shallow your wading pool is.

---

2 In the interest of accountability and modeling what I want you to do, at the end of this book I've placed a list of the titles and a brief description of those books I would like to write.

3

Setting

All good stories are placed in the backdrop of the setting. So, here's the backdrop/setting that got me here.

Weird

I'm a middle-aged white man who grew up in the middle-class south in a quietish town. I played sports, took piano lessons, and argued with my parents about curfew. I was never scared for safety (except when I was in places I had been told not to go), never lacked for needs (although I had plenty of wants that went unfulfilled), was given the chance to try lots of things (and discovered I wasn't very good at most of them), and got exposed to lots of people who weren't like me (and I liked most of them). I got a college education, a decent career path, and eventually married someone from a family similar to mine.

But somehow, I thought my upbringing was weird.

Normal

My son went to college and came back with this observation: "Dad, we're so (pause) normal." When I asked for an explanation, he said, "Most of our family isn't divorced, we aren't chasing some scheme, we have everything we need, and no one is crazy, in jail, or overdosed on drugs." We didn't tell him everything, clearly. But as he interfaced in a very diverse college environment, he realized that being "normal" isn't all bad. It afforded him opportunity and protection that gave him freedoms. He has a sensible view of right and wrong and the internal fortitude to make choices to avoid disastrous consequences. You can call it privilege. In my family, we call it upbringing, love, and good decision-making. And I see it across any color of skin, country of origin, economic status, philosophy, or orientation. There is an opportunity to make something of our lives. I think it's mankind's greatest and overriding desire: to matter. That thought alone is probably a future book.

There is more than a subtle hint from the media and modern culture that my background and the life I've had should make me feel guilty. I don't deny that the path to make something of myself has been easier than what many people face. In fact, I've stated at every turn that if I don't do something at least moderately important with my life, it would be a great shame and poor reflection on me. Greatness isn't reserved for the privileged, though, and the leap to do something magnificent has so far escaped me. I have far more respect and admiration for those who come from humble means and accomplish great things than those who have stories and background like mine who wade in mediocrity.

On the negative side, adherence to standards was important in my world. From parents, neighbors, teachers, and the community at large, you were expected to conform to the culture. And I did. Mostly. That gave me a positive reputation, even though internally it may have caused me to be a bit of a rebel at heart. When I failed to live up to the expectations of others and myself, it was devastating emotionally. I think, like most people, my view of myself and the view others held of me were starkly different. While it may never be fully settled, I was well into adulthood before I was comfortable with my identity, preferences, and purpose.

4

Organizing Deep Thoughts

One of the central themes in developing content that I've adopted from my life as a speech coach is that the human brain craves organization. Even for artistic folks who think in the abstract, a system of organization is what the brain uses to file, recall, and build upon.

But that creates a problem with Deep Thoughts. They don't always appear in context. I can be listening to a podcast on time management and hear a quote that causes me to think deeply about relationships. I can be in the middle of writing (maybe about Deep Thoughts) and have an AHA! moment about the construction of a particular word, which causes me to look it up and discover some never-before-seen (by me) Latin root that puts everything into a new light and needs to be included in my next class on public speaking. A measure of music can spark a memory that reminds me of something I heard a friend say decades ago and lead me to look in my old yearbook and spend an hour reliving the past.

So when you end up with several thousand words of random

Deep Thoughts, it's hard to imagine how a reader would make any sense of them, stay interested in reading more, or have any chance at remembering anything you write for more than ten seconds.

Unless . . .

The author organizes them in some way that your brain can follow, file, and remember.

I originally thought this could be sort of a page-a-day calendar, or a Deep Thoughts Day-by-Day, with 365 entries. I thought about making each month a theme. I thought about putting them in alphabetical order (not sure what value that would have to anyone other than a librarian). What I settled on was topical. I suppose you can make this an inspirational devotional and read each entry on a separate day if you like. Or drop by monthly to see what's next. Or plow through the whole book in one sitting. Or open the pages randomly. Your choice. You, the reader, are in control of consumption. I, the author, am in control of the presentation. I've decided to organize my thoughts based on larger topics and themes that I think are important for leaders and Deep Thinkers to get right. They also happen to be the topics that take our thought and time, and the ones that most people, at some point in their life, have serious questions about. These categories are my attempt to organize my Deep Thoughts and provide you with an organized roadmap so you can choose your own path for reading.

- Relationships and People
- Habits and Behavior
- Time
- Work and Money
- Stuff
- Death

- Legacy
- Mind and Emotions
- World Problems
- God

But then as I tried to put my notes into these categories, I ran across several collections of thoughts that had their own themes and found I needed more categories:

- The Beach
- Near-Death Experiences
- Questions (without Answers)

5

Relationships and People

I'm not a counselor, and I don't play one on TV though I often wish I had some background in human behavior and therapy. Because relationships are the one thing we can all count on having to navigate. And they're hard to get right.

Friends offend us and we move on. Families can't agree who should get Grandpa's old shotgun and never speak again. Coworkers avoid each other and gossip maliciously in the breakroom. And lovers who commit their lives to each other sometimes walk away.

While relationships are complex and include such factors as upbringing, personality, pain (of all types), world view, and the phase of the moon, they are part of the human experience and worth figuring out.

The soil of love

While working with a program designed to bring a city together[3], we were creating curriculum around what we called The Seven Grand Oaks of Community (Arts, Athletics, Business, Education, Government, Health Care, and Non-profits). We used the metaphor of an oak tree to describe the development of dreams and how they matured. We needed a way to wrap up the program. The question was asked, "What makes a tree grow to maturity?"

The answer: the soil. But what is the soil of a community that makes all aspects grow into a healthy function? Our answer: love. But that term isn't batted around much in a community. The program head has a definition for love that makes this work.

Love: sacrificial giving for the benefit of another.
–Wes Simmons

Love makes any relationship work. When my behavior is geared for the benefit of another, then the relationship is on the right footing.

Looking for love

A friend had his first baby. Well, his wife did. The birth had some complications, and the birthing mom was whisked away to ICU. My friend got a handsome dose of reality that this

3 I had the privilege of working with 3D Institute on this project in St. Joseph, MO, for several years and still use their methods in my teaching. You can see the ongoing story at www.thejosephcompany.com.

needy new soul was looking for things he could not provide. And it wasn't just milk.

Psychiatrist Curt Thompson says it this way: "We all are born into the world looking for someone looking for us." The newborn, from his first breath, is looking for, needing, someone to love him. It isn't hard to realize that this need doesn't go away when we are weaned.

Fastest delivery ever

I heard the quote "We all are born into the world looking for someone looking for us." on Father's Day. I was researching it. Had Dr. Thompson's website up on my screen. My bride walked in and saw his book jacket and said, "I've heard a lot of people mention that book." Two minutes later, she came in with a gift and a "Happy Father's Day!" I opened the box, and it's the book I was researching. She said, "I read the description and it seemed like it was written for you." Haven't read a word yet, but the meaning of the book will be secondary to the meaning of the gift. Someone knows me well enough to find a book written for me before I had ever heard of it. Someone loves me. She's a keeper.

Say it (or else!)

I was in a doctor's office waiting room. The receptionist was on the phone, presumably with her bestie, speaking in a voice that was far too loud and giving me (and everyone else in the room) complete access to her side of the conversation. She was complaining about her boyfriend, or maybe her husband.

Whatever his title, he wasn't living up to her expectations. One particular line caught my attention. "How many times am I going to have to say 'I love you' before he says it back? He needs to get it together."

Now my guess is this guy's refusal to say "I love you" was not his only transgression. He probably acted selfishly, ignored her needs, was at times demeaning, and left the toilet seat up and the toothpaste cap off the tube. But the refusal to take a hint or respond in kind was too much for his significant other.

There are several errors of communication here. First, the expectations were not clearly outlined. I'm guessing that culture and upbringing factor in. Perhaps the young man grew up in a household where articulating love verbally was not done, or maybe his household was so dysfunctional he wasn't even sure what love was. Or maybe he didn't love her. Second, when he failed to meet expectations, a gentle reminder to him, not the girlfriend and a waiting room audience, would be a positive step forward.

Navigating a love relationship is hard. It's making yourself vulnerable, admitting that a petty vice (to you) is a big deal to the other person. Sometimes it seems easier to bury it and deal with it internally, creating potential delayed conflict.

As this conversation showed, buried feelings and hurt come out somewhere. In this case, in a waiting room.

W.A.I.T.?

Overheard a conversation in an airport. It was not hard to do. The chairs were right on top of each other. This guy was sitting within a few feet of me. It was hard NOT to hear him.

He was striking up a conversation with people he didn't know. They were students.

He started with the delay of our flight. "Ridiculous. No reason for it. They could easily have made things happen faster."

Within two minutes, he was randomly railing on people with an Ed.D. degree. "Useless. All they do is sit around and create problems. Can't do anything but teach."

Then he moved on to COVID. Doctors. Politicians. People who read the internet. According to him, they were all idiots. He knew a better way.

I wondered what the new friends he was talking to thought. I imagined for fun that one of them was taking aviation management, another was finishing up their Ed.D., and the other was completing a degree in epidemiology. Then who would look like an idiot?

I also realized I've been guilty, many times, of the same behavior. Offering an opinion or a criticism of a large group to someone who didn't ask and likely could be offended by my comments.

Sometimes it's best to keep your mouth shut. I can't believe I just typed that. (Remember, I make most of my living by speaking.) Here's an acronym that haunts me:

W.A.I.T. - Why Am I Talking?

More airport quotes

This was on a plane, waiting to take off. Guy behind me was talking his fellow passenger's ears off. He said, "All I need is coffee." Then quickly, "And Jesus." He went on to quote, "All things work together for good." He notably left off the second half of the verse he was quoting ("For those who love God and are called according to His purpose.").

Then he announced that he'd been smoking pot and had a bad migraine.

I put in my earplugs to drown out the noise and offered a prayer of thanks he wasn't my seatmate. If he had been, I might have said something about sharing uninformed opinions or facts about Ed.D. degrees or COVID and taking care not to offer Bible quotes carelessly.

We broke up

In one of the public speaking classes I taught, the students were remarking on the prevalent use of speech fillers. They mentioned non-words such as "um," "you know," "like," and "literally." Once they became aware of the use, they began correcting themselves and others on this annoying little habit (that is remarkably easy to fix, but that's covered in books I've already written).

On day two, I typically ask what they observed in their evening relative to the skills we're discussing and practicing. One man said he called his girlfriend and noticed that she used a particular word in every sentence. He finally got the nerve to point it out. A large argument ensued, and he told us the relationship ended that night on the phone, instigated by an observation of a speaking tic.

I initially felt bad, thinking I was somehow responsible for their demise. But my feelings quickly moved to pride, thinking that I had saved this couple from a horrible existence had they chosen to continue the relationship.

Good relationships can handle observations and discuss and power through them to a better future together.

Contrast that relationship-breaking observation to a woman in our class who "smacked." She began every sentence by smacking her lips. She went home after day one and told her husband, who said, "I know. You've done that ever since I've known you." She got mad and offended, wondering loudly (by her account), "Why didn't you tell me?" His response should go in the lover's Hall of Fame and be a lesson for all of us who aspire to love better: "Why should I? It's part of the woman I fell in love with." That's the affirmation someone who has just had a painful realization about herself needs.

I don't know how the story ended or whether it was a good or bad ending, but when the student came back to me for a follow-up class, she burst through the door and exclaimed, "It's gone!" When I asked what she was talking about, she said she had eliminated her smacking. I assume her husband was okay with that.

Best friend

One day on my morning walk I passed a woman wearing a shirt that read, "Most of my best friends are animals." My first thought was "It must stink to be you."

I'm one of the few people on the planet that never had a pet growing up. I kept tadpoles for a week before they all died. I toted lizards around and even played with roaches in my bedroom (I grew up in Florida). My mom would have gladly welcomed a four-legged child into our home. Dad wanted nothing of the sort. He had grown up on a farm and apparently had had his fill of animals.

Later in life, I married into a dog family and had a couple of matching chocolate Labrador Retrievers. While they were a joy to have, they were also a lot of work. In my older, more crotchety years, I've swung more to my dad's view. I will often tell people I have a favorite breed of dog: other people's dogs. I love dogs, but I don't want to live with one. (Nor cats, sorry. I'm allergic.)

I watch people adore their pets. I watch a society that reveres animals, their treatment, and their emotional benefits. And I love animals. But animals aren't people. And we were never intended to have our best friend be a dog, I don't care what the adage says.

It strikes me that the view that says a dog is man's best friend (650 million results on Google) is one of selfishness. I can get all the things I want out of a relationship but not have to put up with the sacrifice and complexities. If I'm kind, the tail always wags. If I feed them, I always get a frenzied response. They don't react badly to my swings of emotion.

That all sounds great, and it is. But it's not the level of intimacy that we were intended for. And if your best friends don't include two-footed animals, you're missing the great intent and reward of humanity.

A-list (and B and C . . . and F)

In a debriefing with a friend, he said, "I need to be more consistent about catching up with Chad." The consultant in me kicked in. "What would be the desired frequency to catch up?"

The answer for this person, for this friend, was there needed to be weekly contact. We all have friends like that, where if we go a week without catching up or touching base, the relationship feels out of sorts. When they have a need, we drop whatever we're doing and attend to it. They are a priority. We NEED these people. I call these A-list relationships. Our immediate family most assuredly needs to be on this list. We probably have a friend or two that should be on there as well.

Then there are friends we love and cherish, but don't need to see or hear from regularly. When they call, we answer. If they ask us to do something and it's convenient, we do it. But if we can't get to them, or don't hear from them, it's not the end of the world. We'll make an effort, but we don't HAVE to make the connect. Call these our B-list friends.

Then there are people who are maybe more acquaintances than friends. If they call, we might call them back. Or not. We might reach out to them. Or not. We might agree to meet them for lunch. Or not. It's not that we don't like them. It's not that time with them isn't pleasant. They just aren't a priority. Our C-list.

Then, there's those people. The ones that drain us. The ones we know if we answer the phone it'll be an hour or more of our life that we'll never get back. Perhaps we feel obligated to take the call. Perhaps it's pity or duty. Whatever, these are draining relationships. And too much of them can leave us tired, frustrated, and perhaps even angry. Call them F-list. We need to minimize how much we allow those on this list into our lives.

As I contemplated this model of relationships, I realized it's okay to recognize that all relationships are not created equal. We don't have to defend or explain our decision not to take a call, not to accept an appointment request, not to rearrange our schedule at the slightest request.

Other side of the call

We trumpet and love our personal freedom not to be obligated to other's intrusions to our lives. But when someone—maybe an A-list friend—exercises their freedom, watch out! If the text goes unanswered or the email sits idle without a response, we imagine all sorts of ill has befallen our dear relationship. Of course, we're more likely to call a friend and complain than to ask our friend what is happening, but there's a third solution that is even better.

Forgive and move on. It's doubtful they meant to hurt you. You are their friend.

Relationships change

On the heels of recognizing that there are different levels of relationship, it's also worth recognizing that relationships change over time. Best friends fall out of intimacy and even favor.

A short bit before I began this project in earnest, our best friends moved away. We had known them for the better part of twenty years. Our kids, roughly the same age, grew up together. We vacationed together at least yearly. We celebrated Christmas, New Years, Fourth of July, and birthdays. We found things to do: game nights, plays and concerts, projects and chores. We did them together. They were a phone call and a ten-minute drive away. Until they weren't. The phone, of course, still works. But it doesn't ring as often. We can still schedule vacations together. We've found things to do. But it isn't the same. Sure, we miss them. There is a hole we feel. But life goes on. New friends appear.

Nobody did anything wrong. It's the natural course of a relationship. It changed.

Dad always checks the phone

I will value the people in the room more than the people who are not in the room.

My dad always gets up to check the phone when it rings. With modern convenience, he has caller ID that tells him who is calling. The phone even announces the name out loud. He still gets up to check. Every time. At dinner. From a conversation in the living room. If he hears the phone, he runs to check.

Since my dad grew up in an area that didn't have electricity until he was 12 years old (1946) and didn't have an indoor toilet until he was 16 (1950), I imagine the convenience of the telephone is a special luxury. But in the modern day, it's as much a disruption as a blessing.

I'd guess two-thirds of the calls he gets are "unknown caller" or "suspected spam." I've encouraged him not to pick up those calls. Ever. They'll leave a message if it's important or they'll call back. No reason to waste your time talking to them (or their computer).

But perhaps greater damage is done to our relationships when we prioritize someone not in the room over someone who is. What message are we sending day after day when a live conversation is interrupted by a ringing bell? I've adopted this as one of my core philosophies: value the one in the room.

Apple Watch

When the Apple Watch came out, I was tempted by something new, something shiny. The prospects of answering my phone without taking it out of my pocket, getting news and alerts with a glance, and monitoring basic health were enticing. But my principle with new technology is to buy version 2.0, not version 1.0. Let them get the kinks worked out. Then I'll purchase.

But the kinks in the Apple Watch aren't with the battery life, the view in direct sunlight, or its compatibility and syncing. Those are all fixed (I presume). The kink is with the user.

I've watched friends and strangers with the watch. They cannot help themselves. They must look when it buzzes. Without fail. Check to see who called/texted. Check to see the alert/reminder. Check to update status on heartrate or sleep or steps or . . .

It's taken over their response system. They cannot not look.

I don't want something to control me. I don't want to look away from a conversation I'm in. I don't need an Apple Watch.

Racecars and eclipses

Recently, I went to my very first car race. I'd always wanted to go to one. I still would like to experience a NASCAR race. But this was the local track. Maybe two thousand people there. Locals racing cars they built themselves. The son-in-law of one of my friends was racing. It seemed like a great reason to go.

The track was a quarter-mile asphalt ring. The pits were in sight of all. The local celebrities were out in force.

It was fun. And much louder and faster than I expected. After one wreck, I asked my friend what the repair bill would be. A couple of thousand dollars. But there is no sponsor. No race team to pick up the tab. This Friday night racer would have to pay for that out of his own pocket. It seemed like a lot of wasted money to me. Most of the racers, young men, didn't seem like they would have a few thousand extra dollars laying around.

But I've made this comment in so many areas over the years. There is something that every man would spend his last dollar (and hour) on. If it's your "thing," you get it and support it. If it's not, it seems like a total waste.

My dad never understood sports. "Why would anyone waste their time putting a leather ball through an iron hoop?" He never understood why I spent $60 of my lawn-mowing money to buy a pair of Model 1 Air Jordan's in 1985. (And, sadly, Mom threw those away a few years ago. Cheapest pair today on eBay is over $1,500!)

But my dad has spent thousands of hours staring through a telescope in the middle of the night. He's spent tens of thousands of dollars on equipment and cases, and trips to chase the perfect spot to see an eclipse, occultation, or star alignment. It's the only vacation my mom ever got. They did North Carolina in 1970. Canada in 1972. Australia in 1974. Baja, Mexico, in 1991. A cruise in 1998. Germany in 1999. China in 2009. South Carolina in 2017. My dad has pictures on his wall of each of them. He's been to eight total eclipses, although clouds kept him from seeing two of them. He still wants to see more.

At 89 as of this writing, he has limited opportunities left. He let it be known that he wanted to see the Great Eclipse of 2024.[4] So I made plans to take him from Florida to Texas. He doesn't care about the cost, the time, or the inconvenience. It's worth it.

Like a car to some people. Or sports. Or airplanes. Or writing books few people will read.

"It's easier to let you do it."

My college daughter asked me, "Dad, would you like to vacuum out my car? I don't think it's been cleaned since I got it." It had been well over a year since she began driving "Tracy." I educated her on two things:

1. Her question was flawed. What I wanted or liked to do wasn't likely relevant to the conversation. If she wanted me to do something, she should ask me to do it, not ask me if I would like to do it.

2. Almost every gas station in existence has a vacuum pump off to the side. For a few dollars, she could clean her car most any time.

Her response after a few seconds of thought: "It's a lot easier to bring it home and have you do it."

I expect it is easier. For her.

4 Since writing this, we went to Texas and saw a miracle as the skies literally parted in a short window to allow us a view. Dad was in tears watching his ninth, and likely last, eclipse.

I waffled on my response. On the one hand, my almost 21-year-old daughter needs to learn how to take care of her stuff. It's her car. It's her responsibility. She can't rely on dear ol' dad to do everything for her. She's capable. She needs a constant reinforcement that hard work is intimately tied to results. And life isn't always easy. There are chores and tasks that simply must be done. A car cleaning could be a great classroom to teach all that and more.

But on the other hand, dear ol' dad loves to spoil his girl(s). It's one way I can be sure she gets the message that she is loved and cherished and worth serving. I want her to expect that I will do nice things for her as long as I am able. I know that her future relationships will be enhanced if she can navigate the balance between being cherished and being idolized. She was up against a time and energy crunch that day. Serving her in this way would lighten her load. And maybe it would spoil her.

I not only vacuumed her car, I washed it as well.

Love: sacrificial giving for the benefit of others.

Wife using phone

I had a surgery scheduled. I had a long list of pre-surgery instructions. Shower. Fast. Meds. A responsible adult was required to accompany me. There was only one instruction for the companion: bring a cell phone. I chose my bride to be my responsible adult.

When we arrived at the surgery center, she realized she had left her phone at home. I'll admit I thought (and maybe muttered), "You had one job." But that didn't solve the problem at hand. The solution was easy. She could take my phone.

I would be under anesthesia and certainly had no use for it. She knows the passcode.

I had a slight pause ... she'll have my phone, and access to everything in my life. It was a surprise thought. I guess I've watched too many movies. Then I had a rational thought. There's nothing on my phone that she doesn't already have access to or know. I'm sure there're a few text conversations she would find inane and juvenile, but that wouldn't be unexpected to her. Here, take my phone.

A clear conscience is a wonderful thing.

They even walk the same

When my son was in elementary school, I would occasionally meet him for lunch in the school cafeteria. It was neat to have him pay for my meal (from the account I had funded), to sit with his friends, and choke down the calories they said was food.

One day after checking in with the office, I was walking to his room when I saw his class coming down the hall. I hid behind a corner and when the kids came around the corner, I jumped in line right in front of the boy without saying a word. The teacher began to laugh. I turned my head and heard her say, "They even walk the same!"

I never considered that my son had my gait. I had never mentioned gait to him. Once he learned to motor on his own, I let him do it his way. But apparently he had picked up enough of my habits that his teacher noticed.

It made me wonder, what else have I taught without trying?

Those moments of meaning

It took 28 years of marriage for this to surface. My bride lost her dad unexpectedly when he was 54. I never met him. As our wedding approached, there was a hole in her heart. The man she adored (well, prior to me, at least) was missing. He wouldn't give her away. He wouldn't lead the toast at the reception. He wouldn't be there to put the brakes on spending for the event. He wouldn't crack the dad jokes needed for levity at the right moment.

A bridal portrait had been made, and leading up to the wedding, it was on display at her mother's house with a drape over it. Only a select few were invited to view that portrait before the wedding. I was not one of those select few, but my dad was. When he went to view it, he dropped to his knees and made a huge fuss over the picture. That's not like him, for the record. But he did that in full view of my wife-to-be. And it mattered to her. Deeply. Someone to make a fuss and be in awe and communicate that beauty and love and family and commitment and crazy hot passion were all present and appropriate.

It was a moment that wasn't shared (with me) for almost three decades. But now it's a moment I'll never forget. Not lost on me is that I have a daughter and a daughter-in-law that need to feel loved and made a fuss over and understand family and commitment and the wholesomeness of red-hot passion.

Neighbors

I heard a sermon once where neighbor was defined as "near one." Neighbors are the people you cannot avoid, even if you want to. By that definition, our family is certainly considered our neighbor, as are co-workers and those who live nearby.

In a former day and age, neighbors convened at sunset to sit and talk. My father shares about the men of his community gathering at the general store to smoke and talk while sitting on kegs of nails. The womenfolk were a few doors down, on a screened porch, chatting away.

Every home I've lived in for the last 25 years had a garage. The standard mode of operation is to drive into the garage and close the door behind you. Neighbors speak when they interact at the mailbox, perhaps joining each other for Trick-or-Treating, and may share an occasional meal. But it's an environment that makes it easy to avoid each other.

The command to love your neighbor requires contact. Avoidance is not an option.

Same kind of different as me[5]

I don't know when or how, but, somewhere along the way, I began to be drawn to people who weren't like me. I made friends with people who probably wouldn't have felt welcome in my church. I hung out with people who had a lot less and some with a lot more money than I did. I had the chance to make friends across generations, race, economic status, and even continents. I spent time with and wrote letters to friends and people who needed a friend while spending time in jail. I watched and read perspectives that differed from my own. And I've chosen these thoughts and principles to drive my interactions:

5 Taken from a book (and now a movie) by the same title written by Ron Hall and Denver Moore. It was one of the first books I read as I started my journey to Deep Thoughts. Thanks, Oie, for the recommendation.

- People are far more alike than they are different.
- None of us lives totally by what we say we believe.
- Grace, forgiveness, and a close friend are the secrets to getting through this life in one piece.

If you disagree with everything I write here, we can still be friends. If you hate me because of what you think I'm like, I don't dismiss you.

But here's a Deep Thought that may even be an original one that helps me when I read something that trips my wire.

Truth is truth, no matter the source.

If you're not like me or don't like me or find my views on the afterlife apostate, but I'm telling the truth, well, it's still the truth.

Understanding

It's hard to judge someone you understand.

I don't know the origin of this sentiment. Book. Podcast. Sermon. Conversation. When you dig deep and figure someone out, it's difficult to lump their behavior into a category and judge them. Can't relate to that person with a different agenda, hobby, sexual orientation, or belief than yours? Sit down and ask them questions for the purpose of understanding (not challenging) them.

I remember reading a book where the author related that his

mom had three books on her mantle. I don't remember the specific subjects, but for the sake of making it real, let's identify them as molecular biology, systematic theology, and object-oriented computer programming. They represented the three things her children had chosen for careers. She read books so she would understand her children better, be able to ask better questions, and get in their world. Beats the heck out of "My kids are smart, but I don't know what they do!" Here's another quote, this one from the program I helped adapt from the world of sports to the world of business:

Understanding is the basis of care.

Whether I'm growing vegetables or teenagers, trying to coax a car past 200,000 miles, or re-staining the front door, understanding is the root of providing great care.

Quoting the fifth of Stephen Covey's 7 Habits, "Seek first to understand, then to be understood."

Advice and criticism

It's easy to see the problems in others. We often want to help. And that often leaks out into advice. Well-meaning. Truthful. Good. Advice.

But advice not asked for is seen as criticism. Get permission before you offer advice. An in-the-moment, "Hey, can I share some advice with you?" isn't permission. It's passive aggressive. You get permission with a life of investment, not words.

Let's make up a story!

The missus and I were driving home after our anniversary dinner. In a playful mood and especially talkative, we drove up behind a Subaru SUV with a "chess" bumper sticker at a stoplight. Haley said, "Let's make up a story about them."

We didn't know them or anything about them except they had a normal-looking car and liked chess. Or at least the car owner did. We couldn't even be sure that was who was driving.

The activity was funny. But only because it was easy to do. We stereotyped: drivers of Subarus and people who play chess. Our son plays quite regularly. And then added details that only lived in our imaginations. I doubt much of it was even close to reality.

Which is what we do all the time in our minds about others of all sorts. Make up narratives that aren't true. But if we dwell on them, they become true to us.

I think I'll file that activity in the "Fun, but dangerous" category.

Subaru logo

Random fact that only the son of an astronomer is likely to know: the Subaru logo is an approximation of the star cluster Pleiades (M45), located in the Taurus constellation, just up from Orion's belt.

When I was about ten, my dad took me outside, pointed out the stars, and made me draw the ones I saw. He then compared my card to ones my brother and sister had done with the same exercise at about the same age. A long-distance eye test. I had the best eyes in the family at ten. I no longer do.

Who you gonna call?

Too many times in my life, friends have shared stories that were hard to process.

- Man had an affair with the bimbo (his words) at the office. Told his wife the next day. Predictable results.
- Wife traveled for work, had an affair with a guy on a trip. She 'fessed up. Husband wanted to know what to do.
- Man whose wife of more than twenty years had had enough. They were living in separate homes. He owned that there were issues on his side, took the steps to clean up his life, wanted her back more than anything, but wasn't seeing any progress.
- Man whose private dalliance (addiction) to child porn landed him in a federal prison for almost ten years. Another with the same problem managed to get extradited on the promise never to return to the US.

When I find myself in those conversations, I feel so helpless. I have zero background in counseling. I'm an engineer. Engineers fix things. (Well, we design things, they break, and then we fix them.) I've been told never to offer advice in these situations unless asked. That's a little too black and white for me.

But each of those stories is in stark contrast to the men who never came and told me anything. Like the man who lied to his family about having an affair, lied after he was caught, tried to stick it to his wife in mediation, and continues to lie to his kids about what happened. Or my friend who has had a drink every day of his life since college.

I was in a group discussing the local man who killed his wife and then himself. He missed out on a promotion at work and snapped. In our sleepy little town, it was front page news. One of the details was that he had no friends. A member of our group asked who we would call if life got really bad. One of the comments has motivated me to pursue openness with my friends ever since: "I'm sure every one of you would answer my call, but I'm not sure I'd make the call."

What are we so scared of that we can't share our tough situations? Everyone needs a friend who will listen.

"But woe to the one who falls
when there is not another to lift him up."

Ecclesiastes 4:10

6

Habits & Behavior

In a period of high stress (we were building a house, business was crazy, and we were preparing for our son's high school graduation), things went a bit sideways. Apparently, I got a little hard to live with.

My daughter asked at one point, "Dad, what is wrong with you?" Never one to shy away from the obvious, she was asking what all of us wanted to know.

And the bigger problem was, I didn't know the answer to her question.

Why do we act the way we act?

Environment? Heredity? Culture? Stupidity? Intent?

Yes.

Trip wire

A simple fact: you cannot weigh 350 pounds if you don't first weigh 250. If you allow for the continuity of weight measurement and you took calculus, it's easy to prove. But it's also easy to forget when you're at the buffet.

I ran across a picture of a friend taken about fifteen years ago. I hardly recognized him. He shared he had put on sixty-five pounds in recent years. I wondered to myself when he realized he was overweight. Was it after gaining twenty pounds? Fifty? Or was he waiting for seventy-five to make the declaration?

While losing weight is simple and the process is known to every human in the western world who struggles with weight gain, it is far from easy. I consider myself one of the strugglers. I've battled weight my entire adult life. If losing weight were as easy as it is simple, the weight-loss industry and its $90 BILLION in annual revenue[6] would dry up overnight.

But I have a great trick I've used to keep my weight from ballooning. It's a trip wire. I have a number in my mind that is unacceptable. When the scale comes within five pounds of that number, I go nuts with my diet. I skip meals. I eat smoothies instead of cheeseburgers. I start walking every day. I don't do those actions when I'm comfortably below my number. But seeing that trip wire sets me off.

This technique assumes two things:

6 https://blog.marketresearch.com/u.s.-weight-loss-industry-grows-to-90-billion-fueled-by-obesity-drugs-demand

1. I am weighing myself regularly.

2. I have the will power to stop eating when the trip wire is triggered.

Number two is interesting. I don't possess the willpower to stop gaining weight, but when I get serious enough, I do possess the power to lose it. Odd.

But here's a sobering fact that supports my technique: I've weighed that horrible number exactly once in my life since I've decided on this method. I've hit the trip wire dozens of times.

Wisdom

A definition I ran across for Wisdom:

Wisdom: The ability to see the outcome of our behaviors and adjust accordingly.

It isn't all that hard. Most outcomes of our behaviors are quite predictable. If I drive twenty miles over the posted speed limit everywhere I go, it's easy to imagine what will happen. If I complain about my company (or boss, or salary) to everyone who will listen, it's not hard to envision what my career path will look like. If I consistently tell my spouse they do everything wrong, I can picture what my marriage will probably look like.

Understanding isn't wisdom. Understanding is knowing a tomato is technically a fruit. Wisdom is not putting tomatoes in a fruit salad.

Wisdom involves behavior change. It's doing what is right, as defined by the likelihood of achieving the outcomes we desire.

Defining maturity

A lot of people define maturity in a way that fits their personal habits and situation. I've heard that it's learning from other people's mistakes (how do you measure that?) or the ability to properly manage your behavior (who decides what is "proper"?) My brother shared this definition with me, and it is convicting and accurate.

Maturity is telling yourself "no."

Small children are an example of immaturity. They don't accept "no" for an answer. While this is cute and maybe a great methodology for sales (don't take "no" for an answer), it's a lousy principle to live by. According to this definition, if you want to measure your maturity, identify what you're denying yourself. As I look around, most of America is in the business of NOT denying themselves anything. It's all about me and what I want. It feels good and is easy to order your world when you make it all about you. If I want it, I find a way to get it.

But maturity is about denying those pleasures. We see this in someone who is disciplined. Olympic athletes come to mind. They deny themselves the pleasures of fatty food to give their body the best fuel possible. Those of us imperfect athletes eat pizza. Olympic athletes deny themselves social pleasures to train. We of the imperfect fill our schedules with friends and enjoyment. The elite say "no" to everything that won't further their goal. The normal make decisions in the moment based on their whims.

Before we laud devoted athletes too much, it should be noted that this kind of devotion can lead to hyper focus that wrecks other areas of our lives. It's doubtful many world-class athletes have healthy relationships with anyone other than their coach. I doubt they have time to have many deep, or shallow, thoughts. Whether that is good or bad can't be decided here. I just make the observations.

But telling myself "no" in more mundane and practical elements of life exhibits that I am growing up. Becoming mature. Holding my tongue from that witty remark. Refusing to pack my schedule even though "it'd be fun." And declining that extra scoop of ice cream. All difficult to do in the moment; all profitable in the long run.

Behavior change

Here's a better quote on behavior change:

> Transformation is possible, but it's not inevitable.

Sitting around and waiting for maturity is not likely to produce maturity.

"Oh woe," said to self.

Behavior results . . .

This is another of those quotes I have retained since middle school. I found out later it was a quote from Ralph Waldo Emerson:

> "Sow a thought and you reap an action;
> sow an act and you reap a habit;
> sow a habit and you reap a character;
> sow a character and you reap a destiny."

Life coaches (and sports coaches and speech coaches) focus a lot on actions. But actions come from thoughts. And we have this sort of fatalistic view that we can think whatever we think, but we can somehow change our actions with willpower and effort.

I think this is backward. We should focus on our thoughts, and the actions will take care of themselves.

In his 1902 work *As a Man Thinketh* ... James Allen wrote, "You cannot change your thoughts without changing your life in the process ... either for good or for bad."

Change the way you think, maybe by Deep Thinking, and you will change the way you act without much effort.

Necessary

The pastor of the church I grew up in frequently asked people in the audience to chime in and answer a question. Out loud. With no warning. He was good at adapting to their unplanned responses and working them into his message.

One Sunday, he mused that we didn't understand definitions very well. He announced his intent to call on someone, which he normally did to make everyone nervous. I knew immediately who was going to get called on. I don't know how I knew, but I knew.

"Wyck Hoffler. What's the definition of necessary?"

And Dad, sitting in the choir loft with his chin on his hand, didn't even move or hesitate. His answer was brilliant:

Necessary: Without which you don't.

It's a double negative, consistent with our Germanic heritage. And it's perfect. If something is truly necessary, then you don't do whatever without it.

Was that comment necessary?

Is that activity, expense, trip, or guilty pleasure necessary?

The speed of the farm

My college roommate lives on a horse farm. There is a handmade speed limit sign when you turn onto his quarter-mile drive that reads, "5 mph." The first time I visited (several decades ago), I drove what I was comfortable with. Which was probably twenty miles per hour. Or more. I ate up those yards in record time and wheeled into the barnyard to park. His first words to me were something of the ilk, "My mom is gonna be mad at you for driving so fast." The explanation was that driving fast kicks up dirt, which the horses breathe in, and that causes equine health issues. My young bravado felt that was a bit over the top. Next time I drove in, I kept my speed down, but likely nowhere near the posted limit.

But something happened in the last decade. I realized two things:

1. These weren't my rules, and I wasn't privileged to decide if they were "right" or not.

2. If I couldn't discipline myself to drive five mph at the request of someone I liked, then I had serious problems.

I now drive in at the posted speed. It probably takes me five minutes to arrive. I've learned to enjoy it. It proves to me that I can control my behavior. And I wish my life would travel more at the speed of the farm than the speed of the city.

How do you learn patience?

In graduate school, my friends nicknamed me Mr. P. The P stood for patient. Only it was a backhanded accusation, almost entirely deserved, that I lacked any sort of patience. It was funny, until it wasn't. I knew what I wanted, and I wanted it now. Anyone who dallied was risking wrath.

In testament to the humor of the Almighty—or karma, take your pick—I have been placed in a life where major parts (people) demand that I show patience. It hasn't been easy.

So how do you learn it? Like any other skill: practice.

Pick the longest line at the grocery store. Let someone else go in front of you. Drive behind the slow driver in the right lane and don't pass them. You'll still get to your destination. Don't look at your phone.

All of those activities can develop patience, if you allow them to. Practice.

Practice makes . . .

We've been told that "practice makes perfect." But no one believes that. I teach public speaking for a living. Most people have been speaking (practicing) for decades. No one is perfect. Professional athletes practice all the time. They aren't perfect. And I'm not yet patient, no matter how many slow lines I stand in for practice.

A client in the world of sports taught me that practice makes permanent. HOW you practice dictates the behaviors and habits you display. That's better. But lovely Haley, slow to speak but worth listening to when she does, asked, "Then wouldn't that mean it couldn't be changed?" Ah, she is right. And since my business depends on behavior change, that can't be correct. I had to change my motto.

I found a word my dad would be proud of. Practice makes pertinacious. Extremely or objectionably persistent. Stubborn. Hard to change.

For an easier phrase to understand, practice makes permanent-ish. Any behavior can be changed. But change is hard.

And most people don't like hard. Or want to change.

Sleeping anywhere

One of the greatest results of my bus-driving experience was learning to sleep. I don't know how you learn to sleep, but you had to find a way as a bus driver. For long-haul trips, we would have three drivers for two buses. You drove eight-hour shifts and had four hours off. On some trips this would last for 24 hours or more. If you didn't' sleep, you put passengers at risk.

The buses were loud. There were forty-seven passengers having a great time. The custom buses we drove had tables where people could play cards and couches for relaxing. They also had bunks above the seating. It was a magical design, perfect for youth groups and long trips.

The off-duty driver had access to the bunk right over the active driver. Long before noise-cancelling headsets, I learned to climb up there and fall asleep on a rocking bus, with kids screaming and music blaring. It's a skill I maintain to this day. If I'm still and not engaged in conversation, I can sleep. Quickly. What a blessing (unless you're in the room expecting me to be a great conversationalist after ten p.m.).

Abstaining from ice cream

I love ice cream. It's probably my favorite food. Well, next to chocolate. Or steak. Or a good hearty breakfast. Okay, my favorite food is what's on the plate in front of me. But I love ice cream.

My family grew up eating dessert at every major meal and most minor ones. We had cookies and candy available for snacks at any time. It's amazing we all aren't 500 pounds with blood sugar issues.

But ice cream has always been my favorite. As I've aged and become able to afford the finer things in life, I've adopted a simple mantra: "Life is too short to eat bad food." So I wage a war between the innate cheapness I was raised on with the desire for the best in frozen goodness. I cannot rationalize splurging on the world's best ice cream (Graeter's, and it's not even close)—it's nine dollars a pint. I'll occasionally spring for Public Premium (still a full half gallon). But I mostly settle for what's on sale in a limited set of affordable suppliers (Tillamook is the best, followed by Turkey Hill and a few select Breyer's flavors, notably mint chocolate chip).

In a typical week I'll have ice cream five or six times. As my metabolism has shifted, I've been disciplined enough to cut back on my amounts, now eating from a ramekin rather than a cereal bowl. I never thought it a big deal. Until …

I picked a fight with my coffee drinker friends about their addictions. That's what it is. They can't live without it. They're a different person when they don't have it. It completes and changes them. All words of addicts. So I call it like I see it. They are addicts. And they fight back. Violently.

Their accusation is that I am addicted to ice cream, what's the difference? My reply was always, "I can quit any time. I don't think you can." They didn't see it that way.

One day I decided to give up ice cream. Not permanently, but to prove to myself (and those unbelieving java junkies) that I could. It raised an interesting question: "How long would I have to go without ice cream to prove to you that I could live without ice cream?" No one was willing to tell me how long to go without. They all knew how often I ate it. But we all recognized that a short time (a week) was too little. I'd gone a week without ice cream many times on business or when I was too busy or we ran out and forgot to buy more. I settled on a hiatus of three months. Remember, this was my idea, not theirs.

I happened to choose the three months after a major surgery when I was sitting at home. Those months also encompassed two major eating holidays (Thanksgiving and Christmas). And a cruise.

My friend offered me a deal. I could eat ice cream on the cruise, but it would reset the clock, and I would need to go without the frozen delicacy another three months. I declined.

On the last night of the cruise, our waiter brought me a bowl with several scoops of ice cream. Having seen my appetite for several days, he remarked, "I thought you would like to end with this." He was right. I would have liked that very much. But I was committed. And I passed the bowl down the table to my family.

Lessons from fasting

When I decided to stop eating ice cream, I listened to some teachings on fasting. Odd that in fifty years of church-going, I had never heard a sermon on fasting, other than a historical reference to some character a few millennia ago. No one seemed to be interested in modern people fasting.

Interestingly enough, intermittent fasting is now a very chic activity that is gaining interest in medical and health circles. And my giving up ice cream isn't fasting; that's abstinence. Giving up food altogether is fasting.

But I did learn some things, both from listening and from giving up food(s) I love.

1. You can tell your desires "No." They don't have to control you. Living in the West, we are conditioned to give heed to our desires of every type.

2. Telling the body "No" allows the mind to think more clearly. The rumble in the tummy doesn't last for long and soon you focus on something else.

3. Fasting gives you the opportunity to understand and have empathy for those who don't have a choice about doing without.

This quote caught my attention in my study of fasting:

> Your strongest desires are not your deepest desires.

"I really want it" does not make it a deep desire. Just like a thought is not necessarily a Deep Thought, I guess.

No fruit, no root

Jesus had many difficult sayings. One of them is "Judge not, lest you be judged" (Matt 7:1). Seems rather absolute: don't judge.

But we do it every day. I'm not sure all judgments, by our definition of the word, are wrong.

While I cannot judge a heart, there are three ways I can measure a heart. It's not hard at all. If I want to know what's important to you (where your heart is), I need only to know three things:

- How you spend your money
- How you spend your time
- What you think and talk about

With the exception of our thoughts, these are in plain sight for anyone to see. Said another way, "No fruit, no root." If the tree isn't producing fruit, then the core (heart) isn't healthy.

Identity

In James Clear's NY Times' bestseller, *Atomic Habits*, he states on page 34, "True behavior change is identity change." His basic premise is that you become what you do.

Except for about 18 months when I was primarily a software tester, from the time I was twenty-two years old until now, the only full-time jobs I've held have been teaching jobs. The topics changed. The audiences were different. But I've always taught.

Why then, was I almost forty before I ever came to the point of saying, "I was born to teach"? And how did that realization change my behavior?

When you "teach to make a living," (as I did for about fifteen years), you give minimal effort and find shortcuts to do it more efficiently. You measure success on extrinsic factors like classes taught and bonuses received.

When you "live to teach," you look for opportunities to teach. You find ways to become great at teaching. You can't wait to teach again, and every opportunity helps fuel your energy and satisfaction.

What were you born to do?

Perfection

The word perfection has connotations in our society, both positive and negative. If someone is a perfectionist, that could be a term of derision (they're never satisfied) or one of honor (they value their work and will do whatever it takes to make it excellent). Realists (like me) are quick to point out that we can always do better, so perfection is not a goal that can be attained. Pollyanna optimists will say, "Why not me? Why not perfection?" Others who refuse to examine themselves may redefine the goal so that whatever state they attain is not assessed as "perfect." I heard an athlete say he had to redefine perfection as the pursuit of perfection, not the outcome itself. The word causes us problems.

In the Bible, there are multiple verses with the word perfect (in English) that cause us problems.

"Therefore you are to be perfect,
as your heavenly Father is perfect."

Matt 5:48

"Let us therefore, as many as are perfect, have this attitude;
and if in anything you have a different attitude,
God will reveal that also to you; ..."

Phil 3:15

"And let endurance have its perfect result,
so that you may be perfect and complete, lacking in nothing."

James 1:4

"There is no fear in love; but perfect love casts out fear,
because fear involves punishment, and the one who fears
is not perfected in love."

1 John 4:18

The Greek word most often translated as perfect is *teleios*, but it should probably be translated as mature, or complete. It's the predicted outcome of a path of behavior.

We aren't likely to ever come close to perfection, but we can absolutely aspire to maturity and completeness.

Habit tracking

When I first acknowledged that I was battling a love for food and the fact that love was affecting my shape and weight, I went to a nutritionist. I opened the conversation bluntly: "One thing you need to understand: I love to eat." She laughed and countered with a question: "Are you willing to change what you eat?"

How's that for getting to the real issue?!

"Well, yes. I think."

Her first step was a little education. I loved her example of showing me grapes and raisins in 100 calorie amounts. The raisins were hardly a handful. The grapes were more than I had ever eaten in a single serving. Her point: you can fill up without taking on unnecessary calories.

But her action wasn't "go eat more grapes" (although that was implied). It was, "*Go track EVERYTHING you eat.*" I registered with some app on my phone and keyed in everything I ate. Everything.

An amazing thing happened. I began to eat less overall and eat more of the things that would change my health.

I do a similar exercise with my mentees. I have them catalog two weeks of behavior in 15-minute increments. Phone calls. TV. Sleep. Eating. Deep conversations with their wife. Work.

When they return, I ask them to look at their inventory and tell me what is important to them. It's not a question that is hard to answer with the data in front of them. And I've heard multiple times, "Just the act of keeping track of this changed my behavior."

Same thing works for money. Track every penny. You'll spend less on things you shouldn't spend on and likely save more for what you deem valuable.

Tracking anything changes behavior, for those that care.

Top three best days of my life

My son, a noted lover of reptiles, sent me a video of him taken by his new bride discovering a rattlesnake in the wild. The audio narrative said, "This is one of the three best days of my life!" He was beyond excited. The video noticeably cut out right as he hefted a large rock to throw at said venomous reptile, so I followed up with the question, "What happened?" He poked it with a stick and it slithered away.

But I had a follow-up question that had nothing to do with snakes. "What were the other two best days of your life?"

In my note to him on his wedding day, I told him that sometimes questions were asked that had an obvious right answer. My advice was to always give the right answer.

His response to this particular query was: "Probably my wedding day and something else I don't know." Other than the "probably," that's the right answer.

A snake bit me

Son: I got bit by a snake the other day.

Me: How'd that go down?

Son: I saw a snake when I was playing golf. Fastest black snake I've ever seen. Couldn't catch it, so I tried to get it to strike me.

Success, I guess.

Can't think of a reason not to

When my kids were in elementary school, we planned a Disney Cruise. I had the idea to invite my folks. It wasn't cheap, but they could afford it. It took a commitment, but they were retired. The port was even local to them. Dad said they'd talk about it and get back with us.

In our next conversation, he opened with, "We talked about it. And we can't think of a reason not to go." That Germanic double-negative again.

My friend and I laugh about it to this day. What he didn't say: "We couldn't think of a reason not to go, but it wasn't for lack of trying."

Too often we look for reasons "not to." If it's a good idea, if it brings others joy, if it's worth our time and investment, perhaps we should stop trying to find reasons not to and …

Just do it. Nike and your kids will agree.

Are you a "yes" dad, or a "no" dad?

This humbled me. Thankfully, I found it when my kids were young. I hope I changed my behavior.

When a kid asks something, are they likely to hear you say "yes" or "no"? Both are acceptable. But kids discover quickly whether it's worth the bother to ask Dad. For anything.

I found that too often, my default was "no." No reason. No thought. No explanation. Just "no."

The problem with "no" is that kids will stop asking. And telling. And they'll grow up with a need to tell a therapist at $175/hour that their dad didn't let them have any fun.

You can't read the label from inside the can

This wisdom, via a friend via a podcast, tells us why we're so lousy at analyzing and fixing ourselves. We can't see things for what they are. We're too close to the problem, which is us. But it doesn't stop us from trying.

This is related to another quote I use a lot in the workshops I teach. It's from Stephen Covey, Jr. in *The Speed of Trust*. "We judge ourselves by our intentions and others by their behavior." We may mean well. We may think we're acting nicely. We may intend to come across as likeable and genuine and altruistic and positive and giving and …

But the world can't see those intentions. They interpret our voice, our nonverbals, our micro behaviors, and our macro behaviors and put labels on us. The nutrition label of what's in our package: Selfish. Mean. Short. Condescending. Impatient.

The prospect of that gap should alarm us and drive us to want to know the truth. But to quote Jack Nicholson in *A Few Good Men*, "You can't handle the truth!" Or maybe we don't want it. Because we rarely ask for feedback and often crucify or punish those bold enough to give it.

Put another way:

We are the world's worst judge of ourselves.

Ruts vs. grooves

It's a great feeling when you're in a groove. The zone. In a rhythm. Life happens and the results are good. Could be working out. Good eating or sleep patterns. Date night. Watching the sun set. Efficient practices for time management.

But it's miserable when you're in a rut. Same ol' same ol'. Mundane. Drudgery. Nothing ever changes.

It's worth noting that from the outside, they look the same. When I was mountain biking a little bit, you could see a path in steep turns that all the bikes had taken before. You wanted to pick your "line" and stay in it. But sometimes those lines (grooves) were deep and didn't allow for any correction. A rut. If you got in a rut, there was danger of a spill. Problem was, they often looked the same until you were in them.

It's tough to tell a rut from a groove whether in mountain biking or in life. One sounds like Tigger; the other Eeyore.

> Let's have a date night!
> It's the same date night, over and over.
>
> Ooh, the sunset!
> Same sun, every night.
>
> I need to stick to my schedule!
> It's the same schedule, day after day.

Nothing wrong with repeated behavior. But when does behavior become a habit? When does a habit become a prison? And how can we keep the joy from being sucked from something that we should do?

My three answers:

1. Share it with someone you love. Help them fall in love with it too.

2. Change small things in the big picture. Take a different path home from work. Go to a new place to watch the sunset.

3. Identify (and share) exactly what it is that you like. This isn't easy, but it's effective.

7

Time

It's the one parameter that levels the human experience: Time. We all have the same amount on a daily basis: 24 hours.

We have drastically different amounts in our lives, but that's a parameter we cannot know. We have today.

Time is the most precious commodity we trade in. And trade is exactly the right term. You give up time to spend an evening with a loved one. You give up time to watch a team you love (maybe your child plays on said team, or maybe it was the team that wears a uniform you align with). You give up time to learn, to work, to sleep, to eat, to play.

When someone says, "I don't have time," what they are really saying (but I've never heard anyone actually say this) is, "I've chosen to trade my time for something else."

And, like money, once you've spent it, you don't get it back. Unlike money, you can't make more time. It's the most important asset we control.

QTL

A friend recently introduced me to this acronym. QTL. Quality Time Left.

Most of us live with the hope that our lives will only get better. And in so many ways they do. We typically make more money as we progress through life. We become wiser and make better decisions and become more adept at handling aspects of our lives that aren't good. We develop better relationships.

Physically, we reach a point where it doesn't get better. Our bodies are decaying. Joints wear out. Minds have lessened abilities to function. At some point, life ends.

One thing that is sure not to get better is our QTL. Every day, that number decreases. Your definition of "quality" may differ from mine, and that's okay. But regardless, your QTL today is less than it was yesterday.

I've seen many creative ways to represent this and remind us that today is what matters. An hourglass. A jar of marbles. A countdown clock. Putting a date on the calendar.

I remember a plane flight where I read in the inflight magazine that my life expectancy was 79. At the time I was 39½. Halfway there. It was a seminal moment in my life. Halfway.

The Social Security life expectancy calculator says I can now expect to live to 82.4. Problem is, I'm fifty-six. Maybe only twenty-five years to cram whatever I'm going to do into this life. That doesn't seem like much. Or maybe even enough.

You'll use all you've got

The three major constraints in our life are time, money, and space. We will never think we have enough of any of them. The truth, of course, is easy to say, but it's hard to convince our hearts. We have enough.

This is proven to us when we get more of any of the parameters. When a meeting is cancelled, we find a way to spend that extra time. When we get a bonus or a financial gift, we are immediately struck with what to do with that extra cash. And if you move to a bigger house or get rid of an object, you will find the space is magically filled with something else. Our lives and minds seem to have an aversion to empty space and unclaimed resources.

Say "no"

The hardest word to use, unless you're three, is the word "no." We love to say "yes." "Yes" means people like and need us. "Yes" means we have opportunities. "Yes" means we don't have to make any more decisions, at least for a little while.

But "yes" is, almost by definition, also "no." When we say "yes" to a work conference, we say "no" to a child's ball game. When we say "yes" to a new toy, we say "no" to investing in our retirement fund. When we say "yes" to a favorite outfit, we say "no" to something new and fresh.

None of this is bad. It's just the way the world works.

Toughest time in life

My brother and I wrote a book about the stages in

a man's life.[7] Since we hadn't yet reached the old man and end of life stages, we had to interview those who were ahead of us. One of the questions we loved to ask was, "What was the toughest time in your life?" The answers were amazingly consistent. Not in every case, but in most cases, men (we were writing specifically from the male perspective) said that age 40 was the hardest time.

Perhaps that's because it's middle age. Middle age is hard because you don't have a good answer to the question, "Are you young or old?" My father, now ninety, admits easily that he's an old man. My son, age twenty-three, is quick to confess that he's a young man. It's those of us in between that don't know. The mind says young. The body begins to say old. Society can't decide. Too young to be a church elder, but too old to get the "best up-and-coming" award.

Put the big rocks in first

We've all seen a picture or demonstration of a jar filled with rocks, pebbles, and sand. When you put the sand in first, then drop in the pebbles, and add the rocks last, the rocks protrude from the top. But if you put in the rocks first, add the pebbles (and shake it), and then add the sand, the sand and pebbles fill the gaps.[8]

This is so true with time. I experienced this the summer I was writing this part of Deep Thoughts. I had a lot of small things that got put on my schedule. A client engagement here. A day trip there. A friend who wanted to meet for lunch. An appointment with a repairman. A trip home. A relative that was passing through. When I went to schedule the big

7 *6 Steps Forward*, available on Amazon

8 I wrote and spoke about this on my web site: https://onlinestagecoach.com/stage-coach-blog/b/big-rocks-small-rocks

three-week vacation we had been dreaming about, there was no three-week block available. Such trips need to be put on the calendar well in advance and before all the smaller tasks and requests come in.

This prompted me to make an Annual Plan that included the Big Rocks for next year before the small requests can come in. When a client asks for a date, it's easier to say "I'm not available for those three weeks" and make adjustments from their end. And if they can't adjust, well, I'll be okay. As a friend told me, "Saying yes to everything to make a buck is a good business strategy . . . for a startup."

Daily non-negotiables

A consultant friend works with his clients to get them to identify what he calls the "Daily Non-negotiables." The DNN. In the parlance of the last entry, these are the big rocks for our daily lives that cannot be moved. Perhaps it's eating well. Exercising every morning. Beginning the day in meditation or Bible study. Giving good time and attention to a family member.

They are non-negotiable. They will happen. I love the term. My guess is we all need to add some things to our DNN list. Life would be better for the effort.

What is soon?

I love *The Chosen*, the mini-series about the life of Jesus and His disciples. It gets criticized for telling stories that aren't in the Bible. Which is ironic, because it's never claimed to be a documentary of the Bible, and in the Bible itself it says there were lots of stories that occurred that weren't written down.[9] But I digress. Full disclosure: my wife and I were extras in *The Chosen*, Season 3, Episode 8 – we were part of the crowd of feeding the five thousand (and a spoiler alert/ insider information: there were only 4,000 in the crowd).

I admire the writing. It's easy to follow and listen to. It's funny. It's enlightening and thought-provoking.

At one point, a disciple asks Jesus if something is going to happen soon. Christ's response, "What is soon? Six days we try and master space. We take one day to master time." It's a nod to the Jewish custom of Sabbath, where they put all their work into six days of the week.

It's all about perspective. How you view time.

It's comical to watch young children try to master time. Christmas is coming soon (three weeks): for kids, "It's never going to get here!" while parents scramble to get packages delivered on time.

But adults struggle as well. "I thought I was going to be promoted soon after the project." But you didn't know the timeline for promotions, so you can't say if it was soon or not.

Soon can only be tracked in the face of expectations. The truth is we don't know anything for sure about the future, so "soon" cannot be assured.

Live for today. It'll happen ... soon.

---

9 John 21:25

Wild inefficiency

In researching a talk I was giving, I ran across a web page titled, "Changing Times."[10] It was an analysis of surveys that reported how Americans spend their time and how that has changed in one generation (2003-2016). It should probably be noted this is about the same time the internet exploded.

Of particular note:

- Education drops off. Apparently, we find different ways to learn (or we are learning less).
- Way more time engaged in household activities. These homes we love aren't havens of comfort. They are time sucks that demand more and more work.
- Leisure. With all the promises of more time to spend doing what we want, we actually do less of what we want.
- Shopping. We shop less but consume more. Perhaps we buy, instead of shop. It's easy to click "Add to cart."
- The thing that tops almost every survey for what's important—family—comes up as a declining activity.

My guess is that we all succumb to something that contributes to these statistics. It's only through analyzing our own behavior that we can beat the norm. The statistics sound

10 https://graphics.wsj.com/time-use/

horrific, but it's our behavior that creates these statistics that matters.

When life works best

A friend gave me this phrase designed to analyze what we do and figure out what contributes to life going well. That could be defined as efficiency (for you Type As out there), happiness, stress-free living, or fulfilling purpose and significance. The goal is to identify what makes life work well and plan and pursue those things.

Years ago before I was introduced to the concept, I began tracking (in a spreadsheet, the uber-tool of all tools!) the things in my life that I felt were worth tracking. It included the hours I spent in various types of work, recreation, and things that were important to me. I didn't have the language, but I was making my own When Life Works Best list. A few things are obvious to me:

- I value time with the people most important to me. Perhaps the most treasured line on my spreadsheet is "Family Meal." (*Side note: I began tracking this when my kids were in high school. The most we ever had in a year was 168—less than half of our days gathered around our table. Disappointing.*)

- I track sunsets and sunrises. It's one of the best things I can do with my time. I've generalized this to "get outside." My days are better when I spend some time in nature. Even if it's pulling weeds (I try to take a lap around the house every night in the summer), I need to get outside. COVID and the computer part of my job conspire against me.

- I track time watching TV. And I "don't watch TV." For a guy who "doesn't watch TV," I was shocked at how much TV I watch. I read the average American spends over three hours a day watching TV. No wonder our lives don't amount to much. I average about a half hour a day, split evenly between sports and movies. I don't watch ANY syndicated television. I can always think of so many other things I would rather spend my time doing. Of course, some people can't imagine spending time watching a sunset, either.

- I track days I've spent time reading (and specifically, reading the Bible), playing the piano (a great soothing place for me), and eating out (for a guy struggling with his weight, this is a clear indicator of where the problem originates.)

My dad modeled this tracking for me. He has over fifty years of data on what he eats, how much he sleeps, and the phase of the moon (he's an astronomer). I don't think anyone will ever read his (or my) data, but it's by tracking When Life Works Best that helps us design and live the lives we want to live.

You have to pause to look

The quote below got my attention given my love for sunsets.

> All the glories of midday are eclipsed by the marvels of sunset.
> — ***Charles Spurgeon***

I'd love to know what inspired Pastor Spurgeon to say

such a thing. Had he had a great sermon that morning? Had he ministered to some parishioner? Had he attended to chores and been particularly productive? Had he eaten a fantastic meal? The "glories of midday" are what we aspire to every day.

But Spurgeon was faced with an even greater glory. That of the sunset. I agree. Whatever we accomplish is trivialized in comparison to a sunset.

But the sun sets every day. Clouds obscure many sunsets from my view. But my schedule and the hope to continue making glories of midday are more likely to keep that setting sun out of sight. I'd have to stop what I was doing.

Last afternoon I got a text from my bride. "There is a pretty rainbow out." It was out. Outside. Out my window. But I was in. Inside. In my office. I can't be inspired by that beauty if I don't look, or go, outside.

Marvel at beauty. Seek it out. Take it in. Compare the rose to your to-do list. Put your dashboard next to the sunset. Hold up your bank statement in front of the mountain. And watch the eclipse.

The date

It was sometime around the first day of kindergarten, August 28, 2006. I was reveling in how fast those first five years had flown by and how natural and wonderful and sad and bittersweet it was watching my firstborn head off to school. And it hit me. There's another date coming. I couldn't know its exact date, but I made an estimate and chose August 19, 2019 (8-19-19). It was the approximate day that I would drop off that same boy at college, assuming that was the path he chose to take.

That date changed almost everything for me as a parent. I was no longer parenting for Today; I was parenting for The Date. After The Date, he would make decisions without asking my permission or telling me where he was going. After The Date, his actions could be completely hidden. After The Date, he could try, do, or be whoever he wanted to be.

A large part of me feared that day. I'd seen firsthand what happened to some unprepared classmates that first week of college. Many of them never made it to the second semester. I'd seen habits formed that would take a lifetime to break. Or never be broken. There is a lot for a parent to fear about the life of a college freshman.

But there was another part of me that loved the thought. He would be free and independent, which is what every young man wants. He would be on a path where he could discover what he liked and didn't like without the pressures of a prying, and caring—let's not forget caring—parent. He could meet new people and try new things and alter his course and have the time of this life. All good things.

But my challenge now was to prepare him to make those decisions in such a way that he'd reach adulthood with a positive experience. I had twelve years. Twelve very short years. I'm so grateful for the perspective The Date gave me.

It's time

I missed my estimate of The Date by two days: it was August 17, 2019. The last few months, especially after high school graduation, had been tough. I adopted another mantra: We can no longer live in the same house. It was time for him to go.

A friend told me that the teenage years were God's gift to parents to make them ready for their kids to leave. Seems about right.

He left. He made great decisions. We welcome him back now with anticipation and joy, along with his wife, whom we adore. I'm writing this on Father's Day. It is hard to express how much joy I receive from thinking about my children.

8

Work & Money

One element of human existence is the use of time, effort, and talent in the world of work. Even if you were born into riches and don't need to work for money, you'll find yourself engaged in some activity for the purpose of productivity. Next to sleep, we'll spend more time engaged in work than any other single activity in our lives. But those of us who live in a world where we can work to provide for our needs and have a little left over tend to focus our lives on the time outside of work, not the time we spend on work. "Workin' for the weekend" isn't just good '80s music, it's a mantra that has invaded our society, affecting our work ethic and motivation to produce.

Trading time for money

My first full-time job after college was teaching high school. I had no experience teaching. I convinced my old high school administrators that I wanted to make a difference in kids' lives. They hired me. But I still had to teach.

Since I didn't have any past years' lesson plans to fall back on, I spent long hours preparing my lectures for the next day. I don't think I was ever more than one day ahead. The work required long hours. When I also accepted a coaching position, I was putting in sixty to seventy hours a week. Given my annual salary of $22,525, I was making less than $10 an hour. My coaching supplement added another $5 an hour.

Later that year, the city I lived in found out I knew a few things about computers and a department hired me to set up their CAD system for one of their workers. They paid me $300 for the installation. I worked maybe three hours. I was good at math. It became obvious to me that I didn't need to trade time for money. I didn't have the ability to work enough time. Later this would be a key principle of my pricing strategy in my business.

Sell value, not time.

My job is . . .

At one point in my career, I worked for America's largest privately held software company. When I left, they had over 15,000 employees. They made over two billion dollars a year. The primary owner was the richest man in my state and the 104th richest person on the planet.

In answer to the "What do you do?" question once, I said, "My job is to make a rich man richer." At the time I was frustrated with my own lack of progress, low earnings (in my opinion), and frustration with my job assignments.

It turns out with a few years of perspective and running my own business for fifteen years, that was a great answer. It's exactly what I should have been doing. That's what he (through five layers of management) hired me to do. There aren't many other reasons to hire an employee.

It is called work for a reason.

My job is . . . part deux

For more than fifteen years, I've owned my own business and made a living through whatever income I could cobble together. Once the income leveled out a bit, I began to hire tasks that I didn't want to do or couldn't do well. In almost every case, my employees were quick to tell me what they were weak at.

I'll admit my hiring process was less than thorough. I hired good people I liked, not experts for the task at hand. I expected there to be a learning curve. I was hoping that learning was part of why they wanted to work for me. I figured by the time they learned to be an expert, the job would have changed anyway. I was right.

In many cases, it was a great experience for both parties. In a few cases, the challenge was too great. I've had seven people come and go in various roles.

I recently hired someone new. He gave the same tired line. But I've learned a bit, too. My job as "the boss" is not about task management as much as it is people management. So I spend more time asking what makes them tick and how their motivation is holding up than I do what module of our web tool is crashing.

A competent, motivated worker will find a way to do a task well. An expert without drive will find a way to complicate a task and do the minimum to get it out the door.

Do what you love

Perhaps no statement has changed the American work landscape more than, "Do what you love and you'll never work a day in your life." I don't know when this originated, but we now have a generation who has grown up hearing that. I think the damage inflicted by that mindset is pretty great.

I'd rather we pushed the narrative, "They call it work for a reason." Or "Nothing worthwhile was ever easy."

And I say this as one of the fortunate ones who has had careers that gave me a handsome living while not being particularly onerous. My first job, teaching high school, was my toughest (and least-paying). So everything after that has been easier with greater financial reward. I LOVE what I do in the business I own. I have very few bad days as a result of work. Lots of hard, long days, but few bad days. But there are still elements and tasks that have to be done, or I don't get to do what I love.

I was prospecting a potential employee once and we were discussing compensation for the various elements of serving a client (the sale, the delivery, the development of the content). He made the comment, "Well, if I'm doing the hard work ..." referring to delivery of the material (we're a training business).

No, that's the billable work. The hard work is getting a web site, brand, and marketing strategy set up (because I don't like to do that). The hard work is writing proposals and landing the deal. The hard work is billing, accounting, and cash flow. The hard work is balancing new technology with what is currently working. The hard work is researching ways to make the product fresh and applicable and extending it to a wider audience. The hard work is staying on clients' radars so they think of you when they have need and money.

The hard work is what you don't want to do and what doesn't come easy. The hard work lets you do the easy work and get paid for it. And usually, the hard work is what makes a business successful.

Falling behind

I have a member of my extended family who works in high tech. He's reached that middle age part of life where soccer practice and piano lessons and committee meetings at church make for very busy weeks.

I asked him how work was going one day, knowing full well the rest of his life was full and his line of work is demanding. He said he had made a conscious decision to prioritize his family. I applauded his decision and told him so.

But he also confided that there were young, hungry, incredibly competent workers who were pushing him. They didn't have families and kids and mortgages. They were willing to work long hours. The thrill of being on the bleeding edge of technology was fun for them. They saw the carrots being dangled and understood the rewards ahead. His comment got my attention: "I'm losing ground to them every day. They'll catch me at some point, and it'll be too late for me to recover. I'm going to ride this as long as they'll continue to pay me."

This is both refreshing and alarming at the same time. It's refreshing because purpose and principle were in front of prominence and paycheck. But it's sad because the fire is out. There is no drive to excel. It's the golden handcuffs of a well-paying job that doesn't demand more than he was willing to give.

I've got options

In the last few years I was at The Firm, money was tight. We had small children and a lot of obligations, a house that had more than its share of expensive problems, and we couldn't seem to forge ahead financially.

I decided to moonlight, partly because I needed a new challenge, but I was also motivated by the lure of having a little extra cash. I started businesses, hired myself out for contract work, did odd jobs, and did some writing for pay.

None of my side work made any real dent in our budget. I did manage to cover my startup costs for a few electronic toys I bought to start businesses. I remember bragging at the time that I had "options."

Then I went to a conference for my real job where Jim Collins (*Good to Great*) spoke. He said he had a full-time job and also was working in his think tank. When he met with his mentor, he bragged about how he had two good options for his future. His mentor told him, "As long as you don't commit to one or the other, you'll never be great at either." Jim quit his job, became a famous author and consultant, and never looked back. That speech felt like it was given specifically to me. I began divesting myself of distracting side gigs to focus on what I had the best chance of turning into something great.

What am I good at?

When I was going through my first midlife crisis at about age thirty-nine, I was asking myself what I was good at.

What I was created to do. I took tests and assessments and asked anyone who knew me well what they thought. It was an agonizing time, because I couldn't relate many current activities to things that gave me joy or that I was good at.

I asked my wife what she thought. She rarely answers such questions without time to think, and this anecdote may be the reason why. She blurted out, "You're better than anyone I know at talking until you figure out what to say." She meant it as a compliment. As someone who spoke for a living and was getting into teaching speaking for a living, it seemed like an indictment of narcissism. Now, I advise others not to speak until they know what they want to say. Silence is a virtue. Pauses are your friend. But I didn't do that well at thirty-nine.

The positive spin to that was that I had acquired a skill, without realizing it, of adapting on stage. It began when I took a job I wasn't qualified for as a teacher at age twenty-two. It continued as a college instructor, was given a little structure as a corporate trainer, and honed to a knife edge in corporate America as a consultant needing to give instant answers and coaching to a variety of situations and people.

It's a bit like the Karate Kid. I didn't, couldn't, know at the time that I was being prepared for a bigger task. But when I needed the skill on big stages with important people, it was there. Sometimes what we're capable of isn't obvious until we need it.

Wax on. Wax off.

Party question

One of my favorite party questions is this: "If all jobs paid the same, what would you do?" A small minority of people say, "What I'm doing now." And I don't believe most of them.

But the power of the question is separating the job from the reward or compensation of the job. Psychologists would refer to this as intrinsic motivation: you do what you do because of the joy of the task, not the reward of what is given for completing the task.

Most of us don't have the luxury to "do what we love to do." But there are elements of any job that can be enjoyed simply for the task at hand. Focusing on that can bring us joy even in the midst of hard or boring work.

If wasting time were a profession . . .

I heard this in a men's room at a flea market. Dad remarks to his son, who was ostensibly washing his hands, "If wasting time were a profession, you'd be a millionaire!" It did make me chuckle, only because my son was no longer that age and in that pattern of life. But that child was.

But then it made me want to cry. What message did that little boy hear? Perhaps he was watching the spigot splash and was destined to be a fluids designer, crafting boat wakes that would entertain millions. Maybe he was trying different speeds of water, destined to design a new spigot that would save millions of gallons of clean water. Maybe he was distracted and thinking of a person he had just seen and had a heart to serve as a counselor. There were all sorts of professions he might have been training for. But the message to the son was clear, at least to me. You need to do what I want you to do, and making money is of prime importance when you trade your time.

There are a thousand better comments to make in a men's room or elsewhere to your son.

People do what's important to them

It's a statement I hate to make and hate to hear: "I don't have time." The reality is you always have time. You just chose to use it on other things.

This thought could apply to money. "I don't have the money." No, you spent your money on something else. I'm not talking about buying jet planes, but the decisions of disposable income and time.

A friend and I run men's retreats to get men to examine the core elements of their life. When it comes to time and money, we teach that it's a vote on what's important to you. People find a way to do what they love. People find a way to finance the activities that they love. They find a way.

It's not that you don't love whatever is in question, it's that you love or want something else more. It's not wrong. But don't try to tell someone that you didn't have time for them or for an activity.

Same for money. We drive a fifty-thousand-dollar pickup and take a week-long vacation to the beach every year, but we tell our kid we can't afford to put her in dance lessons.

The difference between obsession and commitment

I'm writing this on a very bittersweet day. I'll be watching my dear daughter-in-law play softball. It could very well be her last day playing. Ever. If it's not her last day, then the opponents on the field will have several members playing in their final game. Softball is going to end for a lot of people today. And if not today, then at most two weeks remain in the season.

The life of a D1 athlete is far more rigorous than most people know. At a small, unrecognized brand program in a sport only the parents (and parents-in-law) care about, the athletes work EXTREMELY hard. Twenty hours per week. And that's in the off-season. It's nearly 24x7 in season. Or 24x6 if the NCAA asks.

The coaches demand an unreal commitment. But at what point does that commitment become manic? Where does the pursuit of excellence become an obsession? Where do we draw the line between a noble pursuit and an idol?

The answer lies in the heart. Purpose. Motive. Discussing this with a group of friends, I got a response that sports doesn't end with nothing. You get friendships, discipline, and resilience. But those things are rarely talked about. I watched my favorite hockey team end their season two nights ago. I can't find an article today about their friendships or their teamwork. Only what they need to address in the offseason and how expectations weren't realized and that some players stunk it up and need to be cut or traded.

Today, the realization is tangible in my family: it's going to come to an end. For everyone. Perhaps the trophy is raised. More often it is not.

I ended my competitive basketball career crying in a locker room, having fouled out in a loss to end a 3-22 season.

I ended my active non-competitive career on an operating room table. It ends poorly for everyone (not named Peyton Manning, I guess).

I asked my son what he remembered about his last game. "Grounded out to the second baseman. That's it." The recency effect[11] suggests that we remember the last thing more than anything else we encounter or learn. But there was so much leading up to that at-bat worth considering.

The Deep Thinker will realize this isn't a thought about softball, baseball, or basketball. Your work is going to come to an end. Your marriage is going to come to an end. Your life is going to come to an end.

Did you idolize the outcomes (which is likely to end in disappointment) or work for something greater? Even if you win the trophy, what next? No one in middle age cares about your state championship in high school.

May I ever be reminded:

"Whatever you do, do your work heartily, as for the Lord rather than for men, knowing that from the Lord you will receive the reward of the inheritance."

Colossians 3:23-24

11 Look it up. It has a Wikipedia page.

9

STUFF

Because I live in America and have always had access to a job, I've also had access to money. Which means I had the ability to purchase stuff. Whether it is necessities like food and clothes and toilet paper, first world "necessities" like cars and media subscriptions, or hedonistic desires like a woodworking tool or a jet ski, the allure of stuff is alive and well. Raised in a household to be extremely frugal (some say "tight"), as my buying power has increased, so has the tension of where "stuff" belongs in my life.

That tension makes me think. And all too often, these thoughts end with the realization that stuff doesn't really matter. And yet I still consume.

Cleaning out the minivan

An earlier entry alluded to the fact that keeping cars clean is not a high priority in our household. Cars are transportation to us, little more. But there does reach a point where sanitation and health become an issue if there isn't an effort to beat back the mess.

Donning a hazmat suit, I dived into the minivan with a trash can and a Shop-Vac at the ready. Full disclosure, the hazmat thing was for dramatic effect. I was dressed for summer work: shorts and T-shirt.

I managed to pull the following out of our 2002 Honda Odyssey:

- A steering wheel cover (not on the steering wheel)
- Two boxes of wet wipes
- A can of Fix-a-Flat
- Three umbrellas
- Two towels
- Masks (this was before COVID)
- Grocery bags
- Nine unopened bottles of water
- A windshield shade
- A bag of plastic silverware
- A bottle of hand sanitizer
- A bottle of lotion
- A cell phone holder
- A tube of Chapstick
- Pens. Lots and lots of pens
- A nice collection of coins. I wish I had totaled them. It wasn't a mortgage payment, but it was a nice meal.
- A make-up kit
- A screwdriver
- A flashlight
- A battery
- A bottle of sunscreen
- An expired driver's license

- An expired AAA card
- A vacuum cleaner attachment
- A pair of sunglasses
- A pack of bubblegum
- Several USB chargers
- Several iPhone cables
- A Bible
- A stack of books
- A pair of winter gloves
- A roll of aluminum foil
- A bottle of ibuprofen
- A bottle of vitamins
- Several notepads
- Several buttons
- Assorted membership cards
- Enough coupons to offset the cost of the minivan
- A container of colored sand
- A stack of magazines/catalogs
- Napkins, both loose and packaged
- A bottle of bug spray
- A tire gauge

The menagerie filled a Rubbermaid tub. I doubt any one item on that list is surprising to parents, but when it was presented in its collection, it seemed excessive and out of place.

But upon thinking deeply about the crap in our minivan, I realized that our minivan was more than transportation. It was a library, a collection of information and activities to educate and entertain the young ones entrusted to me while we carted them around. It was a stockroom able to produce needed items at a moment's notice. It was a hospital where physical needs and booboos could be attended to on the go. It was a filing cabinet where printed items could be stored and accessed. It was a toolbox producing a needed implement for a variety of occasions. It was a mobile office where work could be done in the carpool line. It was a financial center, the hub where business could be undertaken on the go. It was a pantry filling the stomachs and needs of a family on the go. Oh, and it was also a mode of transportation.

About that minivan

Like most American males transitioning from single life through young married life into parenting young children, I fought the notion that a minivan would be in my future. Sport Utility Vehicles were tolerable. But watching my close-to-delivery pregnant wife heft a car seat with our firstborn into the safer middle seat of our SUV during the summer put me over the edge.

I had asked hundreds of people about the move to a van. Most acknowledged the social shame and stigma of driving one. But virtually all said it was the family vehicle of choice. I proceeded to shop.

I had never bought a new car before. At the age of thirty-four, I had only had two cars prior to this, both purchased used. Since everyone thought it was the vehicle of choice, deals were not to be had. Used minivans were almost as much as new ones. Most dealers told me, "This is the price, take it or leave it." I was able to find one dealer that would give me $500 off if we ordered online. They would take my personal check and deliver it to my front door. Seemed an odd way to buy a car.

We had it delivered four days before the birth of our second child.

Demise of the minivan

We drove that minivan everywhere. Trips to the beach, Disney, the mountains, and about 4,000 carpool trips (no exaggeration). We changed the oil every 10,000 miles, whether it needed it or not. Eventually, the toll of neglect began to show. The transmission began to slip. The air conditioner wasn't able to keep up with hot summer days. We limped along for several years, making do. A new car wasn't in the budget and Ol' Reliable never left us on the side of the road. But the signs were clear. That day was coming.

I got estimates on the repairs. They came to several thousand dollars. The estimate of the van's value was only $2,500 on the used market without the repairs. We decided to donate the van to a ministry that took cars, fixed them, and gave them to people who were coming out of homelessness into new lives. It seemed a worthy cause, and we could deduct the full value (with repairs) so the tax credit would be equivalent to what we could realistically hope to get by simply selling.

A few weeks after donating the car, we got a statement from the agency. After inspecting our car, it was not deemed worthy of repair and was being sold at salvage. The money would be used to help fund their operation, and we could deduct the proceeds of the sale only.

A car that I allowed my wife and preteen kids to drive around at night wasn't good enough for a homeless person.

Standard of living

The first purchase I remember making was a chess set. I spent my own money, counting out pennies at the register. I recall it was north of a dollar and less than two. I felt so grown up.

But that two-dollar chess set didn't satisfy my cravings. None of my friends liked chess and my older brother could beat me easily, so I tired of my prized possession and set my sights higher. A baseball glove. A book. A GI Joe (with Kung Fu grip!) A letterman's jacket. A video game system (I never got one of those).

Then I reached adulthood as a single man with an income, though meager (I was a teacher making $22,525 a year). A compound miter saw ($175, on sale). A new tent and backpack ($250 total, with a friend's discount). A cruise to the Bahamas ($325). A trip out West to go skiing ($1,100, including food). A new (to me) car ($12,000).

Then adulthood as a man with more income than expenses. A planer and a router table ($250 and $179). A new couch ($1,200). A new minivan ($30,000). An airplane ($65,000)—the worst financial decision of my life. A new house ($335,000). And the dreams of even more. A vacation house (or two). Business property. Investments. Retirement and a life on Easy Street, straight out of Annie.

Don't misunderstand me. I don't spend money easily. Friends call me frugal, tight, stingy. I prefer "responsible." I've never carried consumer debt and love a good bargain and ways to save. I'll wait to satisfy my cravings by saving or sale. Or do without. But the cravings never stop. Madison Avenue has its effect.

The days where a dollar toy satisfies are long gone. Some of the escalation is unavoidable. I pay more in health insurance premiums now than I made pre-tax in my first job as a schoolteacher. My cell phone and cable bills are more than I paid in rent until I was married. The college tuition bill for one semester for one child is more than the cost of my first car.

I once carried my frugality as a badge of honor. I lived for two years in graduate school on less than $15,000 a year. And I never went hungry. I bought tubes of Shoe Goo to resole old sneakers to avoid buying a new pair. I cut my own hair to save money.

I've discovered that the more I am able to spend, the more I seem to want. It never ends. There is always something else to spend money on. Where I once wanted a $2.00 chess set, now I set my sights on a $600 laser engraver, a $1,000 drone, and taking the family on a $6,000 cruise. And I've never stopped dreaming about airplanes. The pull of materialism and the affluent West has me in its grips. And I hate it.

There is only one solution. Really, two.

The first is gratitude. I am grateful I can go to the grocery store and buy whatever I want without the stress of wondering if there is money in the bank to cover it. I still buy the cheapest cereal on the shelf and get store-brand milk because it's 75 cents cheaper than the name brand. But I have never forgotten the days when those decisions were required, not optional.

The more effective solution to combat the rise of a standard of living is generosity. The more I give away, the less power the draw of materialism has on me. I am finding more and more joy in supporting people who have less, giving surprise gifts (sometimes to people who have more), and hosting people and their expenses when I am able. I have never regretted giving, even to causes or people who didn't turn out like I had hoped. Giving frees me from the escalation of more.

Changing net worth

When I went to graduate school, my entire net worth pretty much fit into a Toyota SR5 small-bed pickup truck plus a bank statement that might have snuck into four figures. I'm sure I'll write checks (or scan a credit card) a few times this year for more than my net worth was then. What changed?

Most people alive in the Western world advance their net worth over the course of a lifetime. For those who lived through the Depression, that wasn't the case. But for the last century, it has been.

My dad started his post-home career with only the things he could carry in a single suitcase. He now has enough squirreled away to care for himself and my mom to any reasonable age (thanks to a government pension and frugal saving). And his household items wouldn't fit in two tractor trailers.

Most (All? I can't think of a counter example) of the friends I've been fortunate enough to stay in contact with over the last three-plus decades are in far better financial shape now than when we were in school together. One of the truths I share with my mentee groups (people ten to twenty years behind me) is that they likely will reach a point where money isn't even in the top three of their concerns. That's hard to fathom when you're buying diapers and can't afford to take a vacation.

My obligations, view of money, and expectations have changed. But have I? Ten thousand dollars is still an enormous sum of money.

Buyer's remorse

The fact that we have the term "buyer's remorse" should be an indication that accumulating things will never truly satisfy. But we continue to consume, especially in America. I used to use this topic as a conversation starter in my public speaking classes. But I found it far more interesting to ask, "What is a purchase that you've never had buyer's remorse for?" What expenses, when viewed over time and maturity, are seen as bargains and worth every penny?

I've had a few. My sheet feed scanner. It allows me to dump receipts and documents into it and with the click of a button store them for all eternity in digital format. It lessens my clutter and eases my mind.

Until I got my first smart phone in 2010, I loved every minute of owning a GPS. It could reroute me on the fly and get me to places I didn't know existed. And, as a pilot, it gave me peace of mind I'd always find my way home.

Notably not on the list of purchases I've never regretted is anything with a combustible engine, anything I bought on a whim, and things I bought hoping someone would like me for it.

Shelf life

Every thing has a shelf life. Either it wears out and is no longer functional, or it loses its purpose and is no longer needed.

We should not put our trust in things. Relationships are a far better investment.

The cost of ownership

I saw an article that said the cost of owning an object is usually twice the cost of the object itself. Storage. Maintenance. Upgrades. Time spent on the "thing." The only objects I know that advertise this additional cost are appliances that tell you how much it'll take to power said appliance for a year.

If the price tag showed us that true cost, I wonder how many things we would avoid buying.

Parting with stuff

I blame this character flaw on my parents, specifically my dad. He grew up on a farm shortly after the Depression. They didn't have the money or ability to get new things. So they kept old things and fixed them. They threw away almost nothing.

That mindset was kept through our family long after Dad left the farm. We kept old jars, rubber bands, screws and scraps of metal, old shoes with holes in them, underwear with no elastic, and mismatched plates with chips in them. "I might need that someday," could very well have been plastered on our family's coat of arms.

The sad side effect is that your house (and garage, and attic, and porch, and storage shed) become overrun with stuff. You step over piles of junk to get to another pile of junk to hunt for that object you're sure you saved years ago to avoid spending three dollars to get a new one. I currently live in a house that is about three times the size of my first house. That's a statement both to how I started out and how I've ended up. But the crazy truth is my big house is just as full and packed as my small house was. You'll spend every dime, schedule every minute, and fill every cubic foot.

A year or so ago, my niece spent a few weeks with my dad to help him go through his stuff. He has lived at the same address for forty-six years, accumulating all the while. My niece never lived there. She had no emotional attachment to his stuff. She was raised with a different mindset. She was tasked with throwing things out. And that she did, with abandon.

The attic is clean. You can see the carpet in the guest bedrooms for the first time in decades. Closets have room for clothes. The kitchen cabinets are organized. The garage ... well, Dad didn't let her go in there. His space.

Dad discovered that something he wanted was gone. He could not find the stainless steel cookie sheets my grandfather had made. They were super heavy duty and a family keepsake. Someone at the thrift store got a bargain. Dad wondered out loud what else he was missing as a result of the cleaning spree.

But the other day (now a half year removed from the exercise), he admitted that as more time went by, the less he worried about missing anything.

Stuff only has a pull when it's present. The way to overcome materialism is to get rid of the stuff.

Postscript: The cookie sheets were found in a bin elsewhere in the house a year later. All that disheartened ache for nothing.

What would you do if you found a dollar?

Another in my line of great party questions is asking what you would do if you found a dollar on the ground. Answers vary, but usually center around putting it in your stack of money, trying to find the owner, or spending it.

How does your answer change if we make it $10? A hundred? A thousand? A million? I usually stop when the number gets to a hundred million.

A dollar doesn't change anybody's life, financially. A hundred million is life-changing. But ideally, whatever answer we give for a dollar should be the same for life-changing dollars. It's the principle of how we handle money and allow it to handle us. If we don't have that nailed down, then scale changes us. And more money rarely (never?) changes people for the better.

Cybertruck

As of this writing, I'm up to four sightings of Tesla's Cybertruck. Three of them had attracted a crowd taking pictures and listening to the owner explain the features of his (always a him) new vehicle.

Is it a vehicle or a statement?

Stretch Prius

Driving through my hometown, I saw a stretch Toyota Prius. Someone had taken the time and money to add a third door and extend the body of America's most popular electric vehicle into a . . . limousine!?

I sent a picture to friends via a group text. First response: "So confused. Why would you do that?" Why, indeed. I don't think anyone is clamoring for a party car that seats six and gets 40 miles per gallon.

But it's probably the same reason that people make potato cannons, stainless steel cookie sheets, and racecars. Because they can. And they like it. And they think it will be cool. And they display a part of their soul with it.

The shop where the Prius limo (the Primo?) was parked looked to be a welder's shop. Maybe it was a project for a new welder's certification. Maybe he was given a high mileage car to play with. Maybe someone dared him to try. Whatever the reason, it was one of a kind.

Bumper sticker

Seen on the back of a Prius.

> Cool Prius!
> — ***No one ever***

Guess he'd never seen a stretch Prius.

10

Death

Whenever you think of death, realize this: it's coming for you too. So far, death is undefeated. The Reaper always arrives.

After that pick-me-up, let's think deeper. Though we know for a fact that death is coming, one variable remains undetermined: The Date. Those two facts live in constant tension. We don't think it's today. But we know it could be. What now?

The announcement

Our bodies give it away. For the first two, maybe three, decades, we are growing, getting better, able to do more and more. Then it's a struggle to maintain our fitness, productivity, or progress. And sometime—after forty for sure—we begin to decline. It's the soreness after weed-eating the lawn. The muscle pull when we help a friend move a refrigerator. The slow ache in the back after sleeping on an old mattress at a hotel.

Or worse. A body system fails. An x-ray reveals a bone spur, decaying cartilage, or a displaced vertebra. An oversized prostate. Diabetes. Renal failure. Cancer.

The body announces The Demise. It's usually at a low volume at first. But it gets louder. The announcement forces you to consider two things: 1) you must address the voice to continue functioning, and 2) you will not always be able to function as you have.

The mind doesn't get the message

Though the body sends the signal, it is rare that the mind catches on, at least initially. "I'll bounce back." "It'll get better." And for a time, it does.

When my brother and I interviewed older men for our first book, it was amazing how many of them said, "I don't feel as old as I am." When my surgeon asked me what activities I hoped to regain, my first thought was an activity (basketball) I hadn't played in over fifteen years and realistically could not ever expect to rejoin.

In our youth, the body responds well and recovers quickly. But even as that response dwindles and the body is incapable of returning to its form, the mind still thinks it can/will. It's a tough trap: recognizing reality.

What a way to go

It's a morbid, but interesting, dinner party topic. How do you (not) want to die? Most people agree that being mauled by a wild animal is not the preferred way to go. It's also extremely rare. We've all seen the painful demise when cancer takes a life. No one wants that outcome, but it's statistically very probable for many of us not on death's door currently.

Most people say they'd like to fall asleep and not wake up. Both my grandfathers went out this way. Peaceful. No drama. Just ... gone. Haley's dad died after a strenuous morning of work on an unbelievably hot day. Today, as I write this, is the anniversary of that day. He was fifty-four. I'm fifty-six. Makes me think. Deeply.

I have one friend who says he wants to be a martyr for his faith. Burned at the stake or beheaded. Something to make a statement that this life isn't the end. My friend is in the minority.

But regardless of your preference, the two truths don't change. One, you don't get to choose the time or the method. Two, it's coming.

Assisted living

I've spent most of the last fifteen years making regular visits to my mothers (one birth and one in-law) who spent their final days in "assisted living." Long before we paid a facility to help, there was assisted living through handling menial chores and scheduling. Then it increased to transportation and logistics. Finally, it required dressing, feeding, and bathing. It was hard to miss the parallel to the care of an infant, diapers and all.

Nobody wants to go out that way, relying on someone else to spoon feed them and wipe their butt. The burden on the families is great. Everything else is on hold.

But there's something sweet about that time. My mom isn't in a hurry. She doesn't get upset at the news. She doesn't fret over inflation. Of course, she also sees people in the room who aren't there and can't complete a sentence—at least one that I can understand. My task in her presence is to be there. Rub her back or hand. Feed her. Wipe her drool. All while realizing she doesn't know who I am or remember my visit.

But that's okay. I need the reminder. The reminder that I'm cut from the same genes and am likely destined for the same outcome. While I can hope I go like her father, asleep in a recliner watching a baseball game, it may be that my children spend their inheritance letting someone else powder my behind. Either way, the date is closer today than it has ever been. Time to get busy.

Dying before death

As I inventory the deaths I've been close enough to follow, I note that most people have a decline before they die. Sometimes it's a steady slowing, ending in a shuffling, plodding life that takes half a day to get dressed, fed, and take care of bodily functions. Sometimes it's a drastic disease that takes our function, resulting in a complete reliance on others for even the most menial task. Strokes take memory and function. Heart attacks render activity difficult. Cancer takes an organ, and more. Dementia steals whatever shine was on life.

Those are saddening. It's terribly horrible to watch and experience.

But far sadder is the death that occurs to healthy people. People who lose their will. Who take up space in a recliner when they are perfectly capable of walking. Who mumble in depression when they could converse freely. Who choose to stay at home when they could easily travel.

I don't want to be dead while I'm alive.

When the mind is gone

Recently, public figures have shined a light on mental health. We all deal with mental health on some level.

Both Haley and I faced this with our mothers. Her mom faced physical challenges that rendered her bedridden for most of the last fifteen years of her life. The human body was not designed to lie flat indefinitely. The toll on her body and mind was significant. It was difficult to enjoy her during her demise, even though we could still see glimpses of her former spunky self.

My mom was diagnosed with progressive idiopathic aphasia (the same diagnosis given public attention recently when Bruce Willis received the diagnosis) at about eighty, though she had had issues with memory before then. It progressed rapidly, requiring us to submit her to a memory care unit where she wouldn't wander off or hurt herself and could get practical help with food and hygiene. It is at the point now where she doesn't know night from day, my name or station in life, and can't process steps well enough to dress herself or answer a simple query. She is unable to communicate with the outside world.

How do we process such a demise? The effort needed to sustain these lives is great. There is inconsolable sadness in those who knew the functional life before. My mom was a brilliant woman who could match wits and productivity with anyone. Haley's mother was the life of the party and a glamorous and honorable addition to any event. But in their later years, the people who cared for them knew none of that. They only saw drool, the lack of basic bodily functions, and an inability to control and interact with their environment. My gentle mom swings in anger at those who approach her now. Haley's mom used colorful vocabulary that we didn't know she had and would have never uttered or condoned in her sane life.

What is amazing is that the kind people who care for those with problems don't lament the loss, they just love and care. It's those of us who remember (and care the most) who have difficulty.

I don't dismiss the hardship. My dad had over sixty years of marriage to a woman who completed him and could handle his idiosyncrasies and match his pace and wit step for step. He had lots of better; now he's got a heavy dose of worse. They had lots of health; they now face sickness together. And though their early years were poorer, it's hard to enjoy the richer without the bliss of a mentally well partner.

The challenge is to love. To care deeply. To serve. Not to fix. Cajole. Demean. Just . . . love.

Bad decision, but still gone

There was a news item locally about an 18-year-old killed on the train tracks that ran through my alma mater's campus. I lived next to those tracks for four years, crossed under them thousands of times, and walked down them (although not advised or probably legal) several times.

It's not hard to avoid getting hit by a train. There are only a few trains a day on these tracks. They blow their horns.

They aren't small, so they're easy to see. They're loud. But this kid got hit—and killed—by a train.

It was probably a very bad decision on his part. Maybe some chemical overindulgence was a factor. Perhaps there were headphones or depression or he was acting on a dare. Maybe he tripped and hit his head and was knocked out. It's easy to surmise and offer conjecture. But one thing I know: his parents were heartbroken.

A coworker of mine had shared often about the pain of her young son's addiction problems. He died in a car wreck, drugs suspected to be a contributing factor. I attended the funeral. His bad decisions didn't make the pain of the loss any easier.

It's easy to cast cause-and-effect blame on people who shipwreck their lives. It's harder, and FAR more important, to love those who are affected by those decisions.

I'd rather be known for my love and care of the living than my analysis and blame of the dead.

What of mine do you want?

For maybe a decade and a half, my dad has been talking about dying. One of his favorite questions is, "What of mine do you want?" If he had asked thirty years ago, I would likely have had a long list. But now, since I've been able to purchase most anything I reasonably want or need and have the perspective of how junk accumulates, there isn't much of his I'd care to keep.

There are two things, and I'll probably have to fight for and/or share with my siblings. One is a particular piece of space memorabilia from the moon landings. And the other is his first telescope, which spawned his wonder and began a lifelong pursuit of astronomical photographic excellence.

But more than any thing, I want him to continue to share his wisdom and insight with me. I want him, not his stuff.

11

LEGACY

Regardless of your view of the afterlife, it's clear that our living time here on earth is limited. What's the reason for our existence? Why are we here? Not we as in humans. We, as in you and me.

I believe that born into the heart of every human being is the desire to matter. To make our mark. To have our lives count for something. And those who have aspirations beyond pure hedonism will want that impact to last beyond our eighty-or-so years of life. We'll call that our legacy. What we leave behind. It could be the impressions we leave in those we interacted with, a cause we moved forward or supported, or what people say about us before we are forgotten.

Or it could be a book.

The funeral topics

One of the projects I worked on, 3D Coaching,[12] teaches the importance of recognizing the funeral topics. At a funeral, there are only two topics: The people that they connected with and the cause(s) they were devoted to. I might add a third: the character they displayed.

While the obituary might include their patents, employment stops, and education, the people who show up for the funeral do not care about that stuff. Work? How you treat people is a better memory. Stuff you collected? We'd rather remember the time we spent together. Plus, someone has to get rid of all that stuff after you're gone.

Invest in people. Devote yourself to causes that will outlast you.

Twenty-five years to obscurity

I heard this quote in a podcast: "Twenty-five years after you die, no one is even going to be saying your name." I thought about that. My grandfather died about 25 years ago. We mention him only by title, "Granddaddy." He was a great man, at least in my mind, but a generation later, his name is an afterthought. I doubt my kids even know his name. They never met him.

I asked my dad what he knew about his granddad, who died two years before he was born. Only one thing, other than his name (my dad was named for this grandfather). He ate

12 www.3dinstitute.com. I helped develop and teach a program to get coaches to coach beyond the sport, and then we converted that to a program for businesses to get the most out of their people.

with a knife. Only a knife. Peas, steak, eggs, bread, potatoes. Only with a knife. But we still don't use his name.

You have three options to deal with this information.

1. Be content with your title and recognize that only those related to you have an interest in talking about you after a generation.

2. Do something so magnificent that people will be forced to talk about you years later. George Washington Carver, Eli Whitney, and Steve Jobs come to mind.

3. Be rich enough or important enough to have something named after you. John Deere and Dale Carnegie are examples. But the danger is that you leave a brand and not a legacy.

The after-the-bucket-list list

I heard a speaker on a podcast talking about bucket lists, which were made popular by the 2007 movie *The Bucket List* starring Jack Nicolson and Morgan Freeman. The podcast discusses what people want to do before they die. This becomes a big deal when you have some idea of when you'll die. Most of us don't have that luxury. The opening seven minutes of the movie *Up* share a poignant view of the pain that ensues when we do not accomplish those items on our list. Go watch it.

I've had a bucket list since my mid-thirties. It includes traveling to the Grand Canyon, Israel, and the Lewis and Clark trail, experiences to try (skydiving), business with kids, speaking to an audience greater than 5,000, and acquiring certain new skills (foreign language, woodworking).

The speaker posed the question, "What do you do if you check off all the items on your bucket list?" While I am reasonably sure I'll never get to everything on my list, it's a paradigm-shifting question. He then went on to encourage the listener to make an after-the-bucket-list list. This is the list of things you want to happen AFTER you have departed the planet. Since you can't be a part of the activity, it's about your legacy and your influence. It's more than who gets your shotgun or your first telescope (although it could include those things). How can you get others to continue or pass on your message and values when you're not around?

Hint: you might have to spend time with them and talk to them.

Locations, experiences, and skills are great. But I can't do any of them after I die.

Now is the time that matters to instill and pass along what you desire for your legacy.

Why does making memories matter?

Mom is in a dementia unit. I doubt she knows where she is, the day of the week, or what she had for breakfast. I'm not sure she knows I'm her son when I visit now.

Dad is still very much aware and capable. Which makes Mom's demise all the more difficult to endure and understand. He was lamenting all the things they did that now seem meaningless and the things they never did that he assumed they'd get to. One day. That day never came.

They have a lifetime (sixty-four years and counting) of making memories together. But eventually the day comes when you can't make more memories. And then all the efforts of that life are gone. I can't possibly catalog and retain the memories of my dad (although I'm trying: his memoirs are on my writing list). They exist only in his mind.

Which makes me wonder. Why do we work so hard to prioritize creating memories? I stated that as my primary goal for my kids when I left The Firm. I wanted to create memories. But what will I do with those memories? Lament their passing into a world that can no longer be reached? Double down on a commitment to make new and better and more extravagant memories? Bore my family and friends with long tales and endless slideshows of all the great things and places and people I experienced?

Why memories?

The problem with memories

There are two problems with memories:

1. They are rarely completely accurate. We have a tendency to romanticize or demonize our memories, leaving out aspects that would hurt the narrative around what we choose to believe about the event.

2. They unfairly compete against the reality of today. Since we forget some details or hyper focus on others, remembering the past and comparing it to the present is an apples-to-oranges comparison.

In graduate school, a friend of mine and I would make up country music lyrics.[13] We noted they were almost always pithy, had deeper meaning, and were easy to remember.

13 Side note: country music of the '90s was one of the greatest genres and eras of music in history, but I digress.

My favorite made-up lyric (title) which was sure to be a hit single was, "I Miss the Good Ol' Days I Never Had." It's a nod to our poor ability to live with our memories.

A close second in our Top Ten: "Everybody but Me Wants to Date My Baby."

It's never just one thing

An employee at a facility I frequent was "let go." Another employee, telling me the news, was careful to maintain confidence while making it clear she thought the firing was unwarranted. Best I could infer, the fired employee tried to handle some personal business on company time. Justified personal business, perhaps, but personal business nonetheless.

As a Deep Thinker, I nodded and tried to look and sound empathetic. But I also made the mental note that it was unlikely that this singular event resulted in the pink slip. There were other factors. Other incidents. Other shortcomings.

The proverbial straw that breaks the camel's back is easy to blame. Situations are complex. It's always more than one thing.

Retirement

A few years ago my friend, aged fifty-seven at the time, called his financial planner and said, "We need to meet and discuss my retirement." The planner started to give him available dates, and my friend said, "No. Today." It was Friday afternoon and work was not pleasant that day (Or week. Or year.) The planner made time, and they met. My friend announced his retirement to his employer Monday morning, probably more than seven years before he intended. He had had enough.

Rash decision? Hardly. He came to the realization that the stress and schedule and the activity and work he was doing were not what he wanted to be doing. He was fortunate enough to have a way out that didn't include a nine-to-five (or in his case, a six-thirty a.m. to seven p.m.). Not everyone can walk away like that. But more can than are willing to admit.

Another friend announced his retirement date a few years in advance. He made it his sixty-fifth birthday. Another who was a state employee met with the HR office years before his departure and found out the earliest possible date for retirement based on his years of service. He began living on the amount of his pension and retired at fifty-three on the first day of his eligibility. My brother, an owner and senior doc of a private medical practice, told his partners he was ready and asked for their advice. They told him immediately would be good. He sold his shares and although he still works to fill in when they want vacation, he was faced with a blank schedule years before he intended.

It's become my favorite question to ask of my demographic (I'm fifty-six at the time of this writing): "When are you going to stop this work thing?" With the exception of the few examples above, most don't have a date. I'm thinking I should start asking everyone this question. My son recently graduated college and began his first full-time job. It's not too early to start thinking about how work ends.

For most, it's an issue of money. If the 401k or pension or IRAs don't project to meet all the needs (and wants), then retirement isn't an option. I think most financial planners are a roadblock to people's retirement dreams because their calculators include worst-case scenarios and they ask lots of questions that make everything a possibility. You can make decisions in retirement like you do now. Can't afford that three-week cruise? Don't take it. Residual income less than you thought it would be? Don't fund your benevolence (or what will be inherited) quite the same.

But I think most people can (and should) retire much earlier than they think.

As you might expect, it's at the top of my mind right now.

Retirement schedule

I have a weekly meeting with a group of men from church. We've met for well over a decade. When COVID hit, we turned our meeting into a Zoom call, and even after COVID subsided, we kept the meeting virtual to save travel time and allow folks to participate while they are on the road.

Two of the members are retired. We tease them a bunch about their "schedule" and the fact that our meeting is the only day of the week they get up before eight o'clock. Since the Zoom meeting is under my business account, I get notified by email when the first person logs on each week (unless I'm first, which is rare). One Thursday morning, I got an email saying one of these men was logged on. He was first to the meeting.

Only one problem. We meet on Friday.

He didn't even know what day of the week it was. We laughed. But it's a warning to me that I need to retire TO something, not FROM something.

Retire. To what?

The problem with the retirement question for most people is they haven't defined what retirement entails. Your financial planner is going to ask you, "How much money will you need per year in retirement?" It's a good question that is a necessary parameter for their Monte Carlo simulations.

But it's the wrong question.

The better question is, "What will you do in retirement?" Or, "What will retirement look like?"

I don't think I'll ever stop working. As long as I can think clearly (deeply?) and formulate sentences, I expect I'll work with people on speaking better, living a fulfilled life, and delivering teachings on any number of subjects. But I'll be more selective about who I do that with.

I tried to outline what I envision a retirement week looking like. My broad strokes:

- One day writing
- One day coaching individuals
- One day speaking
- One day on hobbies
- One day traveling and adventuring
- The rest: quiet and thinking

Every day: active and moving.

Every day: Making a meaningful connection with someone else.

That isn't a weekly schedule. I might teach three days a week. Or travel two weeks (or more) solid.

Only two of those activities can make me any money. I'd love to be at the place where income could be zero and whatever I'm paid could be channeled to benevolent interests and seeding others' growth. I'm not there yet. Maybe book sales will push me there.

But without the vision of what to do, there is no compelling reason to "retire."

The power of compound interest

When I got my first job at twenty-two, the HR department asked how I'd like to handle my retirement. I have no idea what I told them. I'm sure I did the absolute minimum. Contributing to a retirement account at twenty-two seems like a foolish thing to do. At twenty-two.

I lasted one year at the job, never got vested, and received nothing for retirement for that year of work. But doing the math, if I had put aside even ten percent of my whopping $22,525 salary (about $2,250) and invested it with a decent financial planner in a Roth IRA (which didn't exist at the time), it would be worth almost $50,000 tax-free today, and about $125,000 in ten more years when I'm sixty-five.

Conversely, if I started saving at forty-five (about the time I woke up and started looking at my retirement statements), I'd have to invest that $2,250 EVERY YEAR to get the same return at sixty-five.

Not many twenty-two-year-olds have the extra funds to

invest in their future in such a way. Most sixty-five-year-olds wish they had found a way.

Compound interest in people

The same principle that makes money work makes relationships work as well. Invest early.

I had a neighbor notice that our son, a kindergartener at the time, had nice manners and answered him with "Yes, sir" and "No, sir." He told me, "Maybe I should start trying to get my son to do that."

I didn't tell him the truth. It's too late. Habits are already ingrained. If you aren't modeling and demanding it now, he won't pick it up along the way (unless he joins the military).

It's easy to think that we'll spend more time with people when we retire, or the kids leave, or when this next project is over. But there's no better time than now. And investing early yields the maximum results.

Time over intensity.

Revisiting the cookie sheets

My grandfather was a roofer and metalworker. His work ethic was amazing. I once listened to him give his entire work history, starting with leaving home due to an overbearing stepfather, working in the coal mines of West Virginia, getting let go in the Depression, and signing on with his uncle's business and working his way up in the organization with fifty-five-hour weeks until the day his uncle died of a heart attack. He worked out a way to purchase the business and did quite well as owner for twelve years before he retired and never looked back.

On his death, we found dozens of examples of his handiwork around his house. I have several of the tool trays and stainless steel boxes he made. There's a dirty clothes hamper (that I use for scrap wood in my woodshop). A pair of Rockport wingtips that are seldom worn. His golf-ball retriever: an extendable scoop that he used to recover thousands of balls during his favorite retirement hobby.

Probably my favorite of his crafts are the cookie sheets. They were made from heavy stainless steel, simple in design, tapered on the sides, and imminently durable. There were several of them, and my wife and I were blessed to receive one. Mom (and Dad) had several.

When the sheets went missing at Dad's house after a cleaning spree, it caused a bit of a family crisis.

It's hard to process the emotion of loss over those cookie sheets. On the one hand, I have enough perspective to know that my grandfather's memory is not defined by stainless steel. And even though we loved the memory and practicality of those pans, life isn't measurably changed with their absence. My dad has other cookie sheets that work fine. On the other hand, they were evidence of my grandfather's frugality, practicality, and willingness to serve his family however he could. We all lamented their departure even though they were only flat metal cookie sheets.

Because to us, they were more. They were a tangible reminder of a man who did amazing work at his chosen craft and cared enough to provide for his family.

Version 2.0

I have a friend who wrecked his life. And the collateral damage of his decisions wrecked a few others in the process. He owns it. Bad decision upon bad decision that ultimately came to roost with dire consequences. His circle will never completely recover.

But when the opportunity and circumstances gave him a second chance at life, he pursued it with vigor, direction, boundaries, and purpose.

He sent me an email. I noted his address: name2point0@gmail.com. Two point oh. 2.0 The second edition.

The only reason to have a second edition is to make it better than the first. And everyone has a chance to start the second edition.

Body not shaped like you want? Body 2.0

Job not what you want? Career 2.0

Curb appeal of your house not what you want? Landscape 2.0

Marriage not what it could be? Marriage 2.0 (I'm not suggesting a new spouse, but a new edition of the relationship with the same spouse.)

Most people think version 1.4.2b is the change they need. But changing the circumstances (house, spouse, wardrobe) won't change the outcome if the underlying issues aren't addressed. The 2.0 means a new way of doing things. A new design. A new purpose. And that takes Deep Thinking (and action).

What inheritance?

In the upper middle class that I live in, there is much discussion about how to order your financial world after death. Financial planners ask explicitly about what you're going to leave behind. They joke (sort of) that the holy grail is to die with one dollar left to your name, but no one really believes that. And fewer still can pull it off.

If you have a decent job, live within your means, and invest even a little wisely, you're likely in our society to die with a net worth greater than a buck. What happens next?

For a generation and a half, at least in the circles I run, it's been a foregone conclusion that it will be split and left to the children. Or grandchildren. I watched this happen with my grandparents. One had a fairly significant worth to pass on. One had almost nothing. Regardless of the amount, it was split evenly among the children.

My dad started his career at thirty-four with a net worth of much less than five thousand dollars (a car and some furniture). When he retired with a federal pension, he had enough to pay for care for my mom in her last years of dementia. That is five figures. Per month. For years. The savings will be nearly spent. That's fine.

My life expectancy says I've got about a generation to go, and I'm not done earning yet. But math says I'll likely have something left over—at least on paper—when I depart.

I'd like to think my net worth will not be measured in money.

Estate planning

As I have processed the deaths before me, watched my parents plan for a sooner-rather-than-later demise, and think of my future, the topic of estate planning has forced me to make decisions that seem impossible.

I've seen people with trust funds who bought private jets. And I've watched families never speak again because of a diamond ring that ended up in the wrong hands (or simply someone else's hands).

I've asked everyone I think might have a Deep Thought and read every book I can get my hands on about estate planning. Bottom line: nobody agrees on what should happen. That's up to Haley and me. And I'm not convinced we can completely agree.

Since two generations ago neither of our families had anything to pass on, we're not talking about Bill Gates level wealth here. But there should be something left over when I'm gone.

At one end of the spectrum is the belief I should maximize my net worth and leave it all to the kids. I owe it to the family I may never meet to make their lives secure financially and eliminate the variable of money from their lives. Generational wealth.

At the other extreme is the view that I should give it all away and allow my kids to earn their own wealth, independent of money.

And, of course, any view in the middle or combining those two philosophies is at my disposal.

I have decided to make a few rules about my estate. You can steal them. Or make fun of them. But they aren't shallow thoughts, I assure you of that.

1. Don't create headaches for others after I'm gone. In particular, the executor, trustee, or heir. If they're cursing me on the way to the lawyer's office, I have failed.

2. Don't give beyond what I've educated. Leaving money without instructing someone how to use money is not a gift destined for a positive outcome. Since my kids have left the home already, and I realize I was woefully short in the financial education at home, I've got some catching up to do or I've limited my options.

3. If I am remembered primarily for my financial legacy, then I have failed as a person. That is not what I want to be known for. Use the assets now to create memories and opportunities.

4. All people are not created equal in financial decision wisdom. Some can handle money, some cannot. That must be part of the consideration.

Give it away

From *Radical Wisdom*, a devotion book. July 12th entry:

> The value of life is always measured in terms
> of how much it was given away.
> Whatever you accumulated
> is worthless the moment you die.

12

Mind & Emotions

Perhaps nothing is harder to understand than the human mind. It is complex. Amazing. Capable. Rational. And so prone to lapses of memory and judgment.

Our emotions are intertwined somewhere deep within us. They defy logic at times. They push us to action that cannot be explained. I find it difficult to answer even the question, "How do you feel?" "I don't know" is a less-than-helpful response.

In her most excellent book, *Mindset*, Carol Dweck shows the power of our thoughts in achieving outcomes. An open mindset accepts the possibility of future accomplishment. A closed mindset thinks that the way things are is all they'll ever be. I've read the book several times. I agree with her points. And I still find it nearly impossible to train my brain to think with an open mindset all the time.

From his book *Gun Lap*, Robert Wolgemuth says "We allow our self to talk to us instead of talking to our self." True, but again, knowing the truth and seeing it manifest in our lives are two totally different things.

But I'll choose to at least type with an open mindset; with practice, I can think and act with an open mindset!

Loneliness

The summer between my junior and senior years of high school, my parents sent (allowed?) me to go to Europe with the foreign language club from my high school. At the end of the ten-day trip, I tacked on an excursion to go see the exchange student our family had hosted for a year. He lived in Germany. Our trip ended in Rome, Italy. I had to get to Germany by myself. Our tour guide dumped me at the train station in Rome and off I went.

I had never been on a passenger train before. I think Tweetsie Railroad and Disney World were the sum total of trains I had experienced. The conductor took my ticket and showed me to my seat, which was in a little room with six seats facing each other three to a side. It looked exactly like all the movies. Of course, there were other people in the room riding as well. It became obvious that they weren't Americans on their way to see dear friends. One couple was speaking in another language. I guessed Dutch, but it didn't matter. I don't recall the others, but every seat was full. I was at the window, and as the train began to move and go through the countryside of Italy, I began to feel very . . . alone.

This was in the era before cell phones. No one knew where I was. And to me, it felt like no one cared. I felt like crying, but seventeen-year-old American boys aren't supposed to cry. I didn't fit in with the people I was traveling with. I wasn't sure I would be able to change trains in Munich as was required of me. I had no real confirmation that our exchange student would be there to meet me. (We had only communicated by letters as to the time and place. I hadn't seen him in five years. There were lots of reasons I had to be concerned.) And I was alone.

As I sat staring out the window, I heard a voice, in English. The husband of a couple in my room was talking to me, asking me where I was going. Small talk. I think he may have sensed my anxiety. But he was also alerting me to the fact that it was time to change the room from sitting quarters to sleeping quarters and, apparently, I was in his bed. He told me I needed to leave the little room so the conductor could make the transition. My paranoia told me that he was getting rid of me to rifle through my bags and steal my money.

In fear, I left and wandered to the restroom and up and down the center hall of the train. I'm grateful I found my way back to our room. I took the last remaining bunk, sleeping mere inches from total strangers who likely couldn't communicate with me even had they wanted to. I turned over and cried myself to sleep looking out the window.

Alone.

Later in life I discovered a worse kind of alone.

Worst kind of alone

Far worse than being by yourself is the feeling that you are by yourself when you can look all around and see people. When you ache but have no one to share the pain with. It's the principal problem with social media. You can see others, but you can't share the real you with them.

Dismissing a group

We hosted a small group of three young people who were serving at a camp at our church. They stayed in our home for a week, so we got to know them each evening. One of the young men was a VERY passionate fan of a particular SEC school. In every, and I mean every, conversation, he managed to get the subject to a football game or sports experience reflecting on his beloved school. It became comical. And then tiresome. I responded the way I normally do: with sarcasm. He was easy prey, falling for all my leading questions. I knew enough about college football to needle him about some massive public failures at his institution.

Our daughter had just graduated from high school, and we had posted her college acceptances on the refrigerator. One of them was from the rival school of our guest. He asked about the cards. When we told him what they were, he asked, "So, where is she going?" We told him her choice: NOT the school that was his rival. His response was telling of his maturity, and it took me completely by surprise. "Well, good. I don't think I could stay here if she was going THERE. I could never like anyone from that school."

Really?! EVERYONE from this academic institution should be written off simply by their acceptance letter and decision to attend? The fact that we gave him a great experience and hosted him at our expense would be wiped out simply because of a child's college decision? I didn't tell him I had many family members (and friends) who attended the hated school.

But it did make me wonder. How many great people do we dismiss based on a single demographic data point? The school T-shirt. An accent. One word they chose to use that we would never use. Their hobby.

Not everyone is as their stereotypes say they are.

You can't suppress emotions

"Don't feel that way."

Worst. Advice. Ever.

We are humans. Part of that experience is that we feel. We emote. Our heart and mind coalesce into something we can't explain, describe, or control.

Every morning for the past few years, I've started trying to catalog how I feel. It's harder than it sounds. Some days I'm frustrated. Some days I'm happy. Some days I'm mad. Most days it's hard to figure out exactly how I feel. And even harder to explain. I just feel that way.

It's possible not to feel. It's called numbing. Some people use alcohol. Much of America uses television. Some people pack their schedule so full there isn't time to feel. Regardless, feelings are there. You can't make them go away.

I think there are two better questions than "How are you feeling?" First, "What made you feel the way you're feeling?" And even better, "What are you going to do as a result of your feelings?"

Think and do

NC State University, my alma mater twice over and my employer for many years, has a motto: Think and Do. I still coach the graduation speeches in the business school and almost every student speaker incorporates that motto somewhere in their speech.

It's a decent motto for an academic institution. It implies that thought without action isn't much use. And action without thought usually ends poorly. It's important to recognize the relationship between the two.

Revisit the quote from James Allen: "You cannot change your thoughts without changing your life in the process ... either for good or for bad." The way we think determines what we do.

I heard a man talking about accountability at a conference. He has given his cell phone number and permission to call him to over 100 men struggling with addictions. When they face temptation, his phone rings. He asks them three questions:

1. What are you thinking?

2. What are you doing?

3. What are you thinking of doing?

Consider any temptation: the drink, the allure of fortune or fame, the draw of an attractive person and their flirtations. The three questions will allow us to see where our thoughts might take us before we move. They're even better when they're shared with someone else, before we act.

Emotions are like Deep Thoughts. Best when shared.

Acting out of character

"That's not like him." Usually that's the testimony of someone trying to defend the indefensible. We hear it in courts of law and living rooms. A mild-mannered father of five flies off the handle and chunks a vase at his wife. A logical, pragmatic executive buys a new sportscar with no research. A woman thought to be of the highest character shows up looking like *that*.

In most cases, the statement is true. But it's missing a piece. "That's not like the him he lets me see." Or more likely, "That's not like the him I want to believe he is." Within us all is the capacity to be angry, make dumb decisions, and act in ways that no one around us thinks is normal.

Is the way we normally act who we are? Or is the alter ego who can embarrass our family the real us?

Yes.

You may want to, but you don't

When my grandparents died, my parents were faced with the monumental task of disposing of the physical estate from a distance. They vowed not to leave their kids (including me) with a similar chore.

They failed.

Kids usually fall into one of two camps on most any issue. They either act like their parents, or they vow never to be like their parents. And the decision could be different depending on the situation. Sadly, my house, garage, and attic would indicate I'm a chip off the old block when it comes to stuff.

My career path says I'm very different. My friends and pursuit of fun? Different. Eating habits? Same.

The problem with most of our life-shaping decisions is that we didn't decide them. We inherited them.

Opinions are like butts . . .

Everybody has one, and they all stink. Or so the saying goes. I don't believe that. I love others' opinions, even from smelly people.

I took a personality assessment once that labeled me as one who prioritizes people. Part of that is that I look to get opinions and input from others I admire and trust.

In preparation for this book's release, I mocked up a few covers and sent a note via email to about 30 people I admire and thought would have a good opinion. Here were the voting results:

- Option 1 (a whimsical, bright design), three votes, plus two second place and two "absolutely not" votes

- Option 2 (a darker design with lots of hidden meanings around Deep Thoughts), five votes plus one second place

- Option 3 (a simple, playful design that included a cute baby): Eight votes, one second place, and three no votes.

- I had four people give me ideas and send pictures/designs of their own.

What to do now? There is no clear-cut winner. It was fascinating to read people's explanations. Bottom line: pictures evoke lots of varied feelings. A baby attracts some but seems immature to others. Bright and colorful attracts attention and interest to some and feels whimsical and non-serious to others.

I ended up letting a graphic designer decide. Sure, I had input, but I felt it was better to trust someone with a gift and training who wasn't emotionally involved. It's a special joy and a not-so-small touch of pride to reveal that designer is my daughter.

The challenge for communicators, leaders, and friends is to know what speaks to an individual. You won't catch everyone, but if you catch the one (ones) you want, you win.

13

World Problems

It doesn't take a degree in political systems or sociology to realize that the world has problems. Big problems. War. Hunger. Unrest. Preservation of natural resources. Poverty. Human trafficking. Racism. Disease. I'm sure I missed a big one. Or five.

Most of these problems seem like they should be rather simple to solve. Obvious, maybe. The world has enough food to feed everyone. Why can't we get sustenance to where it needs to be? People are people. Why can't those with differences (language, skin tone, ideology) get along? Is respect and listening too hard to manage?

The answer is equally obvious. People are flawed. Too often selfish. Prone to irrationality. Power-hungry.

When I ponder the big conundrums facing us, it tends to make me lose hope. It's discouraging to think about problems that seem too out of (certainly my) control to solve. What can little ol' me do to solve world hunger? I can sponsor a kid, but that is one out of hundreds of millions. The dent doesn't seem big enough.

But I'm not called to solve world hunger. I'm called to feed those whose mouths I can reach. I'm not called to facilitate world peace. I'm tasked with living in harmony with and respectfully listening to those I come into contact with. I can't cure cancer, but I can love those who are stricken with it. What if each of us took one step, where we are, with those around us to solve the problems of humanity?

Our problem is imagination

Attributed to Andy Andrews, one of the funniest speakers and writers I've experienced: "We put a man on the moon before we thought to put wheels on our luggage." The author quoting him made the observation that our problem is not ability or resources, it's imagination.

I might say the same thing but use Deep Thinking instead of imagination. What could we accomplish if more people were dreaming instead of doing? Sure, it took 400,000 people directly involved with the space program to put a man on the moon. I've seen estimates that one in four workers in the mid-1960s could trace their job directly to the effort. But someone had to imagine that it could be done, and how, before all the work could begin.

"No single space project in this period will be more impressive to mankind, or more important for the long-range exploration of space. And none will be so difficult or expensive to accomplish." (JFK, May 21, 1961, three weeks after our first successful manned launch, a month behind the Russians)

The 99 percent

At one point, there was a loud outcry among Americans to tax, denigrate, and punish the wealthy. Their rallying cry: "I am part of the 99%." The implication was that most of us (I'm in that group) were beholden to a small minority who had more, and we didn't like it. They believed the Golden Rule: He who has the gold makes the rules.

But there was one major oversight in their argument. By the simple fact that these people lived in the United States, had a job, and had the free time to protest what they saw as inequity, they were in the top one percent. Worldwide.

If you have access to clean water, you're better off than 30 percent of the world. If you own a car, you have something 90 percent of the world doesn't. Seven in ten people in the world live off less than ten dollars a day. I spend that on a single meal at Chick-fil-A without a second thought. Well, I do have a second thought: "Add a Cookies 'n Cream milkshake to my order!"

It seems human nature only looks at the imbalance of wealth when we are on the lower side of the comparison. Perhaps gratitude for what we do have is the first step toward solving inequity.

What you deserve

At my niece's law school graduation, the guest speaker made this comment to the new graduates: "You deserve to be happy." I don't remember her name or anything else she said. And I couldn't disagree more with her statement.

I hear similar comments in all sorts of arenas. You deserve

happiness, riches, a good-looking spouse, a healthy body, or that shiny new object. I have come to hate the word "deserve."

The word deserve implies that you have somehow earned the favor of those around you (or the Almighty) to get some outcome. If I work hard for forty hours a week, then I deserve the compensation that my contract spells out. If I break the law, then I deserve the punishment that society says is worthy of the crime.

And we can quickly agree to things that no one deserves. No one deserves to be abused as a child. No one deserves to be stricken with cancer. No one deserves to lose a loved one to the car (not) controlled by a drunk driver.

But deserving outcomes that exist in my mind (happiness) or that help my comfort (riches)? That seems a stretch.

It's one of the great mysteries of life. Why do some people get great outcomes and others do not? In the philosophical world, why do bad things happen to good people (or good things to bad people)?

The answer will elude you, as it has countless millions across history.

I certainly didn't deserve to be born into a middle-class family in the ninth richest country on earth. I also didn't deserve to have degenerative arthritis (genetic) and have both hips replaced when I was fifty-five. But those are facts.

Happiness? I agree with the carefully worded second half of the opening sentence to the Declaration of Independence. Notice the phrase that precedes happiness:

"All men . . . are endowed by their Creator
with certain unalienable Rights, that among these are
Life, Liberty, and the pursuit of Happiness."

You can pursue it. But you may not find it. And all men were not created equal, as the precursor of the sentence states.

You can always give your best

I was fortunate enough to travel to Guyana in 2010. This nation on the north coast of South America is the third poorest country in the western hemisphere. It is most known as the location of the Jim Jones Jonestown massacre in 1978. The poverty there is visible for all to see. The people have little and there is no hope of changing that for most of the population. We ate in a restaurant where chicken cost $11. A gallon of gas was $2.50. I learned that the average income for a family was $2,000 a year. Most families don't eat chicken or have a combustible engine. Simple economics.

Yet when we visited resident homes, they rolled out their red carpet for us. They cleaned. They dressed up. They served the best food available to them (which included meat, something we were told they rarely ate themselves). They even gave us gifts. It was hard to accept their kindness. It felt like I should be giving them gifts and not receiving them.

On the last day we were there, I was playing with some of the neighborhood kids and laughing with a shy preschool girl. Her parents seemed thrilled that the white man would shower such attention on her. Though their English was poor and I spoke none of their language, I got the message through to them that I had a daughter about the same age as this child. The mother lit up and ran into her home. She returned with a toy and a dress to give to my daughter. Based on what her daughter was wearing and the home they lived in, I seriously doubt she had another dress and the toy box was going to be bare upon my departure. She was giving me her best, simply as a token of gratitude for me being kind. I did not want to receive the gift. We both cried as I accepted it from her.

Kindness and generosity are not limited to what we have in excess, but what we have in our heart.

The -20 to +20 model

Hats off to my brother for this one. He presented it to me in 2010 on a porch in the sweltering heat in Guyana, South America, where I accompanied him on one of his more than sixty foreign medical mission trips.

We were discussing the futility of short-term missions and the response most Americans have when they see poverty and suffering on the scale of the poor in a developing country. The realization that our small clinic would only be a temporary respite for a tiny portion of the population and have little long-term effect was humbling. Our minimal opportunity to share spiritual truths or counsel deeply made the feelings of futility even greater. What effect could we possibly be having?

The model says that people are on a journey. At one extreme (-20, but it could be -10 or -100) are people who are lost. Whether you grade that on spiritual maturity, intellectual insight, or on physical health, the principle is the same. Some people are near death.

At the other extreme (+20/+10/+100) are the people who are

at the pinnacle. They've arrived. They lack nothing and are living in the Light. But people aren't born at either extreme. Along the way, there are seasons where we progress and seasons where we have setbacks. If you charted your life, you'd see the peaks and valleys.

In the context of missions, my job is not to get people to +20. If it were, I'd be a failure. I cannot exact that sort of change on a life. In fact, I may not be able to exact any change in another's life. But my goal is to move them along. If I meet a -20, near apostate, radical and militant atheist, maybe by showing love and listening I can get them to consider that not all believers are evil. Perhaps they progress to a -19. Or if I meet someone who is mature and healthy, maybe a +15, I can encourage or challenge them with a new thought to reach for +16. Maybe this book or the idea of Deep Thoughts moves your journey forward toward the goal of maturity.

The idea that I'm not responsible for drastic change to the end goal is very freeing. Instead of trying to fit all my truth and all my ideas into a conversation or chance meeting, I can focus on showing compassion and love and truly understanding where another lives. Forward progress, of any magnitude, is still progress.

Why can't there be peace?

What is it with people that we cannot get along? If you study any period and any locale in world history, it is littered with wars and rumors of wars. In the short (relatively) history of the United States, after obtaining our freedom, we continued to battle. The War of 1812. The Mexican War (remember the Alamo!). The Civil War. The Spanish-American War. The War to End all Wars, followed a generation later by the

Great War (WWII). Korea. Vietnam. Iraq. Afghanistan. It never ends. Or hasn't yet.

Estimates are America has lost over 650,000 service members in our history. That's an average of more than seven people a day for every day we've been a country.

And, depending on which party is in control and the state of world affairs, we spend roughly 40 percent of our total revenue as a country toward "defense." I suppose I'd rather defend our country than be ruled by a despot, but what flaw in human character seeks to take over other countries in the first place? How great a country (and world) could we build if those resources were diverted to solve some of those great world problems?

And the counter argument holds weight as well: if we do not fight to preserve the right to peace, there will be even more world problems.

Why can't we solve the basic problems?

No one deserves to die of hunger. Everyone should have a potable water source. Access to health care. The opportunity of education. Freedom of speech. Freedom from oppression.

Give people these basic rights. Easy in principle. Hard in reality. Three reasons why:

1. It costs. And someone has to pay. If someone (The taxpayer? The parent? The friend?) doesn't want to pay, then it will go unfunded. No funding, no solution.

2. Not everyone wants change, even if it's "better." And who gets to decide what's better?

3. Some people see themselves as better than others. If others are suppressed, it gives power to those who feel superior.

Not one of these reasons is valid enough to withhold basic provisions where need is found. Well, that's my point of view. But that doesn't make my view a universal truth. Or likely to happen.

Someone doesn't live here

My kids throw this back in my face now. But it's a good lesson, and I smile every time they do.

When they were little, I frequently heard "Someone needs to . . . " And my response was always the same: "Someone doesn't live here." If the car needed gas, one of us had to do it, Someone wouldn't. Someone never vacuumed. Someone doesn't know how to cook, apparently.

It's the same issue with world problems. It's easy to say we need Someone to provide healthcare in Africa. It's quite another to be the trained physician—or a helper—who is willing to go and serve the need.

I read a headline about a missionary couple killed by gangs in Haiti after the recent coup. My first thought was, "Why were they still in Haiti? That place isn't safe!" And then I read their organization's statement: "We started Missions in Haiti in 2000 with the purpose of setting Haiti on a different course. We aim to accomplish this by targeting the country's biggest need—its children. Although the entire nation is steeped in poverty, the children suffer the worst. Thousands are malnourished, uneducated, and headed for hopeless lives apart from Christ."

They weren't willing to wait for Someone to help the children in the Western hemisphere's poorest country.

The scale of a government budget

I pulled up next to a truck that was owned by the county I was driving in. It was a NICE truck, much nicer than mine. I wondered why a county employee was driving such an expensive truck. It isn't hard to figure out. There are two factors.

First, it's a matter of math and some Google searching. In the county I live in, there are about 300,000 homeowners (and another 150,000 renters). The mean value of homes is $354,000. This means that the value of residential real estate is more than $100 BILLION. Most people can't wrap their head around the differences between millions and billions (and trillions). But that is an ENORMOUS number. The tax rate in my county is .6570 cents per $100 (0.657 percent). That computes to the average homeowner paying $2,300 or more in taxes on their house. Doing a little math, my county takes in $700 million in property taxes from homeowners. Add to that use tax, corporate tax, and fees. There is a lot of money for governments to manage. Our total county budget for 2024 was $1.875 billion.

I'm choosing not to discuss the morality of their management. I appreciate roads that don't have potholes and teachers who accept low pay to educate our future and parks and programs and libraries and all the rest. The reality is that an $80,000 pickup is a drop in the bucket (.0043 percent of the total budget. They could buy 23,000 pickups every year if that's all they did).

But it does lead to the second factor in why governments

spend so much. I learned in researching the previous paragraph that my county chose not to fund over $100 million in new requests. Departments wanted new trucks (and buildings and staff and copiers and cell phones) but were not granted them. Money, even ridiculous amounts of money, isn't unlimited.

If there's a great shortage in funding, why the nice pickup? It's because individual departments are given a budget and expected to spend it. If they don't spend the money they're given, it will be taken away and given to those unfunded projects (because the truck department clearly didn't need it).

This is a clear difference in the fiscal management of a large organization from that of the private citizen. Many, but not all of us, are fortunate we can be flexible in allocating for expenses. We can shift budget priorities. We can decide not to spend funds now and be assured those funds will still be available later. That's good.

Any organization or department driven to spend every dollar in their allotted budget to retain their budget level will never be efficient due to one simple human flaw: selfishness. They must spend now to have the same or more later.

The pull of more

For all of my life, decisions have had some element of finances to them. Where to eat? Consider the cost. What car to buy? Money is a factor. Where to vacation? What can we afford?

The one financial lesson that was hammered into my brain was to live within my means. My parents did not take on consumer debt and taught me not to. It's a great lesson, and it has served me well. But there's another aspect of importance to financial health. You can earn more.

When money was (really) tight in the early part of my marriage and family life, I took to moonlighting to make extra cash. We weren't destitute. We could pay our bills and have enough for a rainy day. But we weren't making any progress toward larger goals. Some of the nicer things in Western life (new cars, vacations, housing options) were not available to us. But the moonlighting money was "extra." It didn't have to go to a mortgage, diapers, or the gas station. Those things were already handled. It was the ability to buy a half-share in a pop-up camper. A new woodworking tool for a home project. A nicer set of pots and pans for the kitchen.

Our family even managed to make it to Disney World a few times. The Happiest Place on Earth requires lots of extra (and leaves lots of dads wondering if it was worth it). I found myself judging families that didn't appear to have much extra. Inevitably, I ended up judging myself.

The problem with extra, more, is that it's never enough. Make an extra $10,000 on the side and you'll find yourself dreaming about $20,000. There is always something else. When I was in graduate school (where I lived off about $15,000 per year), I dreamed of a backpack, or a new tent, or possibly a ski trip out west. I could occasionally either justify or afford some things I dreamed about, but never all the items on my list. Later in my life, when I was better off financially, there weren't many things or experiences I couldn't afford. But no matter how much I had, the pull of more was always present. A week at the beach is nice, but wouldn't a nice private jet be amazing?! Or owning my own beach?!

The cancer of comparison

I worked for a large company. When I left, there were over 5,000 employees at the location where I worked. That meant large parking lots around the buildings. One day I came back from lunch and had to park far away from the building. As I walked in, I began to look at cars and made a startling discovery. My car was pretty close to the oldest, most mundane, worst car in the lot. I was still driving the first car I had ever owned. It had over 225,000 miles reflected on its odometer, its air conditioner no longer worked (and was an older style that was no longer legal to service), and it burned and dripped oil. It was functional. It had only left me on the side of the road once. But it failed to win a head-to-head comparison with every other car owned by my peers.

That realization caused problems for me that I don't like to this day. I wondered about my coworkers' salaries that allowed them to afford the nice cars in the lot. I began to justify why I needed another, nicer car. And I realized that despite my frugality, I was just as impressionable for nice stuff as the next person.

Sadly, I was unable to deny myself long-term. As summer hit the following year, my justification was that I "deserved" (there's that word) air conditioning in my car. I upgraded to a newer (used) model. But a few years (seven, to be exact) later, I hit a midlife crisis at forty and somehow managed to justify buying a brand-new pickup truck. It was my twentieth year of vehicle ownership and my first new car.

Progress!

The word progress sounds so promising. We've moved

ahead. Getting better. There's even a political ideology based on the word.

Its premise is that mankind will move forward toward a better future. And certainly there are plenty of examples of this in every walk of life. The car gave us access and dominance over space, allowing us to commute to work and see relatives who didn't live across the street. The phone allowed us to have instant communication and get answers to questions in seconds, not weeks. The microwave let us cook quickly and use less effort. Indoor plumbing gave us convenience and did away with the need for a Thunder Jug. I am grateful for those progressions.

But with each progression, something is sacrificed. It may be subtle and almost certainly is justified, but it's still a loss. GPS is wonderful. With its immediate access on our phones, it can get us to our destination quickly, but now most of us have lost the spatial recognition of directional awareness and relative location, the "lay of the land." Follow the magenta line.

With the phone we get instant answers and the ability to connect from anywhere in the world. With this instancy in connection, however, we've lost the ability and joy of writing a love letter and the wonder and thought of trying to figure things out while we wait on an answer. The TV can entertain and inform, but we've allowed it to replace sitting on the front porch and talking with neighbors.

Progress is inevitable. But it comes with a cost.

Lost world

At various times I've reminisced with my dad and aunts and uncles. They grew up in a bygone era. They called a rural farm home. The community probably had fewer than twenty homes. The nearest town has never had a population of more than 400. The nearest town with shopping (a Walmart) is about thirty minutes away. Dad (the oldest) was born in 1934. The youngest of four was born in 1940. They didn't have electricity until after the war in 1946. When they were growing up, they watered the farm animals by toting water from a well. They dug the plumbing for their first (and only) bathroom and installed it themselves in 1950. They had no phone, no internet, no two-way communication with the outside world besides a letter. The family shared a car with the uncle who lived across the street. They had a mule (Ida) and raised chickens to stay alive. They had no money. Everything they needed was obtained by raising it or bartering for it. My uncle said once, "We were just trying to survive." It seems hard to believe those people are still alive in today's world.

While they love their iPhones and their modern pictures and the conveniences of modern life, every time I hear them talk about the lives they experienced, it's clear they miss the old days. Not the lack of an indoor toilet or the inability to buy something they want with a three-minute drive to Walmart. But the simplicity. The work ethic. The nights with everyone on the porch, talking. The shared community values. Those things are mostly just memories now.

From mule to space

I think my grandmother's generation probably had the toughest adjustment of any generation. She grew up pre-Depression with very little in the way of modern convenience. She remembers seeing her first automobile. Her first airplane. I'm not sure she could explain electricity. She seemed to prefer her pump on the back porch to her running water.

As the world changed around her, I can't imagine the mental battles she had to fight. Her son worked for NASA and knew every astronaut that landed on the moon on a first-name basis. She told us she could not believe that the Apollo program was real. Another son flew large jets. All of her kids traveled around the world. I doubt she traveled beyond adjacent counties more than a dozen times in her life.

She abhorred seat belts. They made her feel constricted. She never had cable TV. I don't think she ever saw anything on the internet. I never asked, but I can't imagine how she viewed 9/11 or even if she was aware of it (she died in 2003).

Those are a lot of changes to absorb in one lifetime. They say progress is moving at an increasingly rapid rate, even today. If so, then perhaps my generation will have more to deal with.

What is the next Big Thing that the old-timers will struggle to adopt and the younger generation won't be able to live without? Those that can dream it will benefit from it. Those that consume it will be governed by it.

War is personal, unless it isn't

I remember where I was in January 1991 when I first heard that America had started its attack in the First Gulf War (driving down Highway 50 in my Honda Accord). I don't recall following it much past that first night watching Peter Arnett broadcast live from Baghdad.

I remember where I was when the twin towers came down on 9/11. I remember following the attacks on Afghanistan for maybe a few days. Years later, I barely noticed when it ended.

I remember hearing about the capture of Osama bin Laden. But I didn't follow any of the conflict leading up to or after that event.

I probably could have told you there were wars/conflicts/ actions in Syria, Myanmar, Sudan, and Liberia in my lifetime. But I didn't watch the first clip on YouTube and couldn't have cared less.

But because I had traveled to Kyiv (in 2019) and had friends from (and in) Kyiv when Russia invaded (in 2022), I have followed that war (sorry, Mr. Putin, when one country invades another's territory and people are shooting each other, it's a war) daily and consistently. I scoured pictures looking for familiar sights. I looked at maps to see if where I had visited was affected. It was. I was in Irpin, the suburb of Kyiv famous in the first week of the war showing people crossing a river over a ladder with a collapsed bridge in the background. I had been over that bridge. This was almost personal, even though I lost nothing but time in the conflict.

When you have a connection, you pay attention a lot more.

We're more alike than we are different

Prior to COVID, I had the privilege to travel on a client's dime to Africa (twice), Europe (twice), and Asia. It was my first real experience with varied cultures in their environment. I live in a metro area that is a melting pot, but they're melting into my environment.

Those trips changed my views of the world.

Probably the biggest realization was that people are people. Especially if you level the comparison by economic status and life situation. The middle class in Manila is doing quite well with lots of disposable income and trips to the mall. Families in Egypt want the best for their kids and love following them around in pursuit of sports. Ukrainian entrepreneurs (before the war) were risk-takers who found a way to make a profit from providing goods and services.

Milkshakes first

While I was writing this, my son texted me from South Africa, his first real trip abroad. He said, "In South Africa, every restaurant has milkshakes. And they give it to you before your meal!"

My biggest carnal weakness may be ice cream, and this proves that we can always find some common ground.

Culture dictates behavior

The benefit of travel is getting to see places and people who are different, sometimes far different, from places I know and from me.

One of the starkest examples of the way different cultures behave was the streets of Cairo, Egypt. Our driver picked us up from the airport and warned us. He explained that honking was their way of saying "hello." That wasn't exactly truthful, but it helped us cope.

In most of Cairo, there are no lines painted on the streets. There are no stoplights. Cars, trucks, bikes, pedestrians, and animals share the road. Intersections are mostly roundabouts. A four-lane highway meets another four-lane highway, and the merger is solved by the drivers, not the city planners. Every square inch of pavement is fair for travel. Space between cars is measured in inches (or centimeters). At times it felt like there was no way the traffic could get untangled. But we never stopped, always inching forward.

We observed there were two laws of the road:

1. The horn gives you a slight advantage, if only to distract another driver and give you the chance to inch ahead of him.

2. Whichever car's bumper was ahead had the right-of-way.

It was mayhem, at least to an American. But my engineer mind kicked in, and I had two additional observations:

1. We never stopped. In America, I spend an inordinate amount of time stopped at stoplights and stuck in traffic, even on straight highways.

2. They got more people through an intersection quicker than we do in America, and I never saw an accident.

Our system isn't better. It's different. And traffic systems only work when everyone obeys the same rules. But who made those rules? There are certain immovables, like drive on the correct side of the road. But beyond that, it's taught and learned. People in Boston aren't instructed to honk their horns when a light turns green, but they all do. People in the south aren't given a book outlining the "zipper" method of merging, but they (mostly) do. People in Cairo aren't taught in driver school how to inch a car through gridlock with the narrowest of clearances, but they do.

These are all examples of culture—a set of rules people

adopt to govern their behavior. It doesn't have to be formal or written down. But it dictates how we act.

The more I study and recognize culture, the more I think it is the primary explanation for why we do what we do. Whether it is learned from a family, neighborhood, school, city, state, country, race, income level, or type of work we do, we are assimilated into a culture and our behavior (basically) falls in line.

Side note: if culture is such a powerful force of behavior, then leaders (and parents) would be wise to understand and cultivate culture to get the behaviors they want.

14

God

Here's a subject that's likely to get your attention. Or maybe make you stop reading. Everyone has a belief on the Almighty and everyone thinks they're right. Logically, we can't all be right. Accepting that fact may be the most important aspect of understanding a force or person or entity that is greater than us.

I think everyone, even an atheist, has a god. The one I believe in I refer to with a capital letter—God—and I believe Him to be all-powerful, all-present, all-knowing, all-loving, and outside of space and time.

Other people I've met serve (worship?) the god of science and human knowledge, of fitness and trying to live long, of wealth and happiness, of good deeds and service. Many of those gods make great objects of our devotion, and the outcomes are frequently notable and worthy of human effort.

But none of them solve some of the greater mysteries of life. Notably: how did this whole life thing start and what is my purpose for having life at all? Your answer to those questions probably defines the god you serve. Sadly, most people, including some I've attended church with my whole life, think that answer revolves around them. They are their god.

The great thing about both the belief I hold and the (deep) thoughts I'm about to share is that you don't need to have any agreement with either my thoughts or beliefs to process these thoughts or to have your own Deep Thoughts. Remember, Deep Thoughts are deep because they are shared. So read and listen and think deeply about what you believe. I'm not trying to persuade you to hold a certain mindset or belief. At least not here.

Understanding God

Philosophers have tried to reason an explanation for a supernatural power since the dawn of man. I got this from a newsletter of a friend:

> If we understood God completely,
> then He wouldn't be God.

The only way that you can accept such a Being is to take your views in faith (and if you choose to declare Him not to exist, then you are accepting another set of beliefs and faith). Faith is the belief in something you cannot see. There is much in this world you can't see and yet accept. You believe there is oxygen in the air you breathe. You believe in love and an attractive force to another. But somehow the toughest seems to be a trust in a Being that governs what we wish to control.

The beginning

"Now faith is the assurance of things hoped for, the conviction of things not seen."

Hebrews 11:1

Since I grew up in a house where faith was expected and practiced, I've never struggled to accept the existence of God. But I'm fascinated with the intellectual arguments for and against Him. Many atheists say God is a construct of the human mind, created to appease the dissatisfaction we have with our lives as we endeavor to make sense of our eighty years plus or minus on the earth. There are philosophies that say there is no meaning to those years other than whatever happens during them. This life ends, and with it, whatever meaning and significance we could achieve ends. Therefore, pack in the effort and pleasure, because that's all you've got.

But even if you don't believe a word of the Bible, the opening words must be dealt with: "In the beginning, . . ." One of the great mysteries of life is how did it all begin? The origin of life? Current best guesses include panspermia (the idea that life exists throughout the universe and is transferred through space dust and asteroids). Google's first answer says that lightning struck deep sea vent gasses to create amino acids that then turned into living beings. Another theory says aliens came and left life here (and then presumably departed with no interest in what happened next). But where did the aliens originate? What created the gasses when there were none? And why life? Why here?

The irony of these theories is that they are constructs of the human mind, created to make sense of our existence on earth. That is rarely ever mentioned. Eventually, all streams of thought on the origins of life, the universe, and ourselves lead us to a point of faith. Believing in aliens is faith. Believing in exploding gasses that make life is faith. Believing in an all-powerful God is too. The issue isn't faith, it's faith in what.

God hates tattoos

On an airplane, I saw a man walking down the aisle wearing a T-shirt that proclaimed boldly, "God hates tattoos." He had both arms inked up completely, tattoos on his neck, and, by presumption, tattoos in a lot of places I could not see. He was in a group of similarly-decorated people who appeared to have been part of a tattoo business.

Dude, I've got questions.

Was he declaring that God hates him? Was he being sarcastic and poking fun at God? Was he sticking it to the people who claim to speak for God who have told him he's going to hell for putting ink on his skin (my best guess)?

It does raise questions for the observer. Assuming there is a God, what does He hate? Or love? Or tolerate? Am I on a list? Does God hate tattoos but love the tattooed? Or tattooer?

Does God hate people who say He doesn't exist? Or does He hate people who say they follow Him and then act like the Devil?

God hates cross dressers

I've not seen this on a T-shirt, but I've heard the sentiment. It's come up a bit in the modern cultures debate on gender identity and the choice of children and adults to present themselves separately from their birth gender. Some even quote the Bible.[14] Those quoters rarely continue to the part of the book that includes mandates of mass murder and genocide, which aren't very palatable in the modern era.

I've got a friend who told me he likes to wear women's clothing. If he'd told anyone that four decades ago, he would have been bullied beyond belief. Today, his proclamation hardly raises an eyebrow.

Which leads to an interesting observation about clothing. It's not universally defined by gender. It's a changing definition by culture and era. Scottish men wear skirts. Alpine women wear leather britches. Female athletes wear shorts and jerseys. Wrestlers (and ballet dancers) wear tights.

Who gets to decide?

What God asks of us

Back to The Chosen. One of my favorite lines (from S2E1) is said by Jesus, "I ask a lot of those who follow me. But I ask little of those who do not." I wish that more people would adopt that mantra for their own lives. Many of the problems in this world arise from people asking others to believe, act, and conform to their standards. If you don't believe what I believe, then why would I expect you to think like I do? If your belief system is contrary to mine, why would I expect your actions to conform to mine?

It's so much easier to concern ourselves with the perceived injustices and misbehaviors of others than it is to deal with our own actions. I opened by writing a confession

14 Deuteronomy 22:5

that there are ample visible and tangible ways that my own behavior contradicts what I say I believe. And there are far more contradictions that you can't observe or hear. Any behavior analysis thoughts I have shouldn't be so much the condemnation of others for failure to live up to my standards, but rather the manner of my own shortcomings. And, like most profitable changes in life, this requires Deep Thinking and then, perhaps, changes in action or attitude.

Love

The first Deep Thought of the Relationships chapter was "The soil of love." Love is the soil that makes relationships grow.

For those who base their philosophy on Judaism or its offshoots, it's worth noting that when God was asked who He was, He claimed He was loving and compassionate.[15]

For those who claim Christianity as their north star, love is not an option. Christ said that others would know we are followers by our love.[16] When Jesus was asked what the greatest commandment was, what was more important than anything else, his answer was, "Love." And then he added a second thought and second commandment. Also about "Love."[17]

Love isn't logical or something that can be completely understood. It is the basis for our belief in a Being—or philosophy—that transcends time, space, logic, and explanation. And it allows us to put others before ourselves.

15 Exodus 34:6, Deuteronomy 4:31; 2 Chronicles 30:9, among others
16 John 13:35
17 Matthew 22:37-39

When love isn't displayed

A lack of displayed love is the primary roadblock that many people in the West have against Islam. A "religion of peace" that sometimes makes headlines by sniper fire, detonating a bomb in a crowded market, or all-out war.

There are whole segments of the Old Testament that relate a similar path. And lest we Westerners (and Christians) forget, there have been plenty of Crusades and Missions waged in the name of God (or the freedom from God/god) by people whose statements of faith are not so drastically different from those they condemn.

Wars will continue until Love wins.

I'm a ______ (just not a good one)

Another problem with condemning other faiths based on the actions of an adherent is that very few followers (none!?) are perfect in their obedience to any belief system. I'm pretty lousy at love many days, though I published a Deep Thought advocating for it to guide our actions, small and large. I have Muslim friends who are at least as kind as those of my own faith. I know atheists who do far more good than some people I go to church with.

After many years apart, I met a friend from another era of life who had adopted a rather radical view of his faith, complete with headline-making protests and broad condemnation of multiple people groups. I learned all that in less than ten minutes with him. When he introduced me to his wife, he labeled me as "One of us." I resisted the urge to say, "I couldn't disagree more, but it's a pleasure to meet you" and settled on the last half of the statement. It was, after all, a party, where we were supposed to be happy and all get along. I can't help but wonder if I should have said something to clarify the difference between us.

Not my concern

I've thought quite a bit about fairness. I even taught the concept in a math course when I was a college instructor early in my career. The definition we used as our premise was this:

Fair: Both parties think they got a good deal.

The word comes up a lot. In politics, there is quite a discussion about people paying "their fair share." But when one group imposes the rules on another, neither side will agree. That isn't fair. It may be just, could even be the right way to handle things, but it isn't fair. People, teams, and organizations use loopholes to their advantage, whether that be salary caps, nefarious avoidance of the rules, or enforcing voting boundaries. It's probably legal. It may be borderline ethical. But it's not fair.

But people only seem to call "That's not fair" when they are on the perceived wronged side. No one says, "It's not fair" when the situation benefits them. Rich people typically don't decry the tax laws that protect their wealth as not fair. People who live in a low-crime area don't seem terribly upset by the unfairness to those who can't get out of the part of town that doesn't afford such peace. Farmers whose crops are thriving don't seem to mind the unfairness of the drought or hurricane that decimates livelihoods in another part of the world. Very few people are so altruistic that they wish to give up the unfairness that profits them.

While I wasn't born into what our country would classify as wealthy, we had everything we needed and most of what we wanted. I was given the opportunity to get an education, have a healthy body and mind, and enjoy a peaceful existence. That's not fair. Many people don't have those things. A third of the world doesn't even have clean water.

My solace came from the book *God and Money* by John Cortinas, Gregory Baumer, et al. The authors say that people with such opportunity shouldn't dwell too much on the fairness of what they've got. They say that inequity should not be their concern. They go on to say much about the responsibility for those fortunate ones to do something with the good fortune and wealth they have.

My son said almost the same thing when I took him on a week-long service trip to one of the poorest areas of our country. I think he was fourteen. I asked him how we should respond to seeing such poverty in light of our own wealth. (We were about to go on a cruise and were building a new house.) His comment was along the lines of, "It's not wrong for us to have those things, but we have a responsibility to use our resources for good and to help those who have less."

I agree.

Awe-ful

I love a good play on words. It's especially nice when the wordplay is memorable and poignant.

The word awful is not a middle-of-the-road word. It's, well, awful. Not just bad, but awful. If your day, your relationship, or your health are awful, then your life is not well. It demands that we pursue change to make it better.

But what if our lives were awe-ful? Full of awe. Wonderful. Amazing. Consider each day what would spur us to that wonder. What could we see, hear, or do that fills us with the wonder and joy of a life that is complete? Would a sunset do it? A kiss from our lover (bonus if that lover is our spouse!)? An anonymous act of charity and good?

When we are faced with the awful, look around. Find the awe-ful instead.

The one rule of prayer

From a podcast: The only rule in prayer is show up. You can't do it wrong.

While you certainly can pray for things that likely won't happen or aren't in the will of God (Jesus prayed to be released from His call to death,[18] which we know was not in the offing), the act of prayer is pretty hard to mess up.

Oh, and closing any prayer to any deity you so incline your voice to with "Not my will but Thine be done" isn't bad either. That may be the best verbal expression of love.

Answer the question

A second verse in the Bible that must be reckoned with, even if you don't believe it, is a quote from Christ in Matthew 16. Originally asked of Peter, it's a great question for every human: "Who do you say that I am?"[19] I don't think there are many people left who don't think there was a man named Jesus who lived about two thousand years ago. But who was he? What significance did his life have? Why all the claims

18 Luke 22:42
19 Matthew 16:15

about him? Why such disparate patterns of life from people who claim to follow him?

What's interesting about the dialogue of Matthew 16 is that Jesus first asks, "Who do (other) men say that I am?" It's impersonal. It promotes rumors and tweets and hearsay. It makes for great discussion and debate. Other people say ...

But eventually the real question emerges. Who do YOU say that I am? It's personal. Downright invasive. And there is no way out. No deflection available. No one to pin the blame on or the theory to. It's your belief that matters.

It's easy to talk about others' crazy answers to life's greatest mysteries, but my answers are the ones that should consume me.

Struggles

It's a favorite word of the church crowd. "I'm struggling." Usually, it's in reference to some action that is committed in error (sin) or something that should have been done and was not (a discipline or act of kindness).

But by its very mention, the problem is not knowledge. They knew what they wanted to do (or not do). They just didn't (or did) do it. My middle school youth pastor shared this definition:

Struggle: delayed obedience

Oof. You know what to do. You're not doing it.

I don't say it is easy. If it were, you wouldn't be struggling. But don't talk about a struggle like it's a matter of knowledge.

"To one who knows the right thing to do and does not do it, to him it is sin."

James 4:17

Expectations

A lot of people are mad at God. Usually, it's because the expectations of their life have not been met. Perhaps their (my) expectations are altruistic and even noble. I don't want good people to be punished. I don't like injustice and suffering in the world. I'd like to live in a world full of love and peace. I believe those are wonderful sentiments.

But we get in trouble when that becomes our expectation.

As the wisdom goes, expectations precede disappointment.

Which begs the question, "What do you expect your life to be like?" Did you expect your body to be healthy and youthful, full of vigor and energy right up until your final breath? (Spoiler alert: the body fails and is on a downhill decline as you approach the end.) Did you expect your spouse to be agreeable and pleasant in all circumstances? Do you expect yourself to be? Did you expect your children to be trouble free, always honorable, and celebrated for their amazing accomplishments? Did you expect your loved ones to die without suffering?

For a large part of our lives, things do work out. There is so much to be celebrated and thankful for. But there are those moments, and sometimes they linger for months and years, when things are not pleasant. Relationships are strained. Bodies fail. Finances are lacking. Decisions by those in authority upset and may even inconvenience us. And we don't like it.

But let's bring God back into the picture. It seems that all gods, regardless of their title and customs, are above humanity. They have more power, more insight, more ability. And for whatever reason, they (or He. or She.) refuse to make our lives perfect the way we want. At least on this planet and in this lifetime. Which begs the next question, "Is this it?"

Faith in any higher being, and certainly in the God of the Bible, requires a starting point that God is God and I am not. His ways are not my ways. The standards by which I judge and rate my life are set to different metrics than those set out for the Kingdom of God. His dashboard and mine are not compatible.

Which leads to question number three: "How will I then live?" Will I shake my fist and curse God who refuses to give me my way? That sounds like a preschooler. Will I succumb to the pursuit of pleasure and press on with the things that I think I deserve or that I want? That sounds like a selfish teenager or maybe an unfulfilled adult. Or will I choose to deny myself, trust that God is true and just, and seek to live a life that advances a Kingdom I cannot see for a reward I cannot fathom?

It's not an easy decision to make. And it's even harder to live.

15

The Beach

I don't know what it is about the beach that creates such a positive impression on me (and others). A lot of it probably is that most people only go to the beach for vacation. It's a highly anticipated event, planned for months in advance. The food is good. The recreation is unique. We do things at the beach that we do not, and cannot, do any other time and place.

But a part of the allure has to be the beach itself. Sand. Surf. Sun. We come to brush up against the power of nature with a plan (schedule) that promotes rest and relaxation. Whether you come to fish, surf, bake your skin, eat the seafood, or play beach volleyball, anticipation of a good time makes the beach a place worth going.

I grew up about 30 minutes from the beach and now live about three hours from the beach. I go to the beach now more than I did growing up for a multitude of reasons. But the more I go, the more I love it.

Footprints

A copy of Mary Stevenson's famous poem, "Footprints in the Sand," hung in my parents' kitchen for most of the years I lived at home. Superimposed on a picture of the seashore with a set of footprints set in the sand and disappearing into the distance, the basic premise of the poem is that God travels with us along our journey, and at times, he carries us when we are too weak to walk on our own. It's a touching poem, and the picture gives it gravitas and a visual reminder.

Except it's completely unrealistic.

When I am at the beach, I try to get up to watch the sunrise every day. (*Side note and hot tip: go in the spring, when daylight savings starts and the sun comes up late.*) I walk or kayak a mile or two down the beach, watch the sun crest the horizon or peek through the clouds, sit and ponder life a spell, and return home.

It's a rare day that I'm alone on the beach. I've walked in sub-freezing temperatures and there were others enjoying the coast. I've been on the beach in a nor'easter with winds whipping north of 70 miles an hour and was not alone. There seems always to be someone on the beach, at least the beaches I can afford to visit.

And those footprints. First, there isn't just one set of footprints. One of the things I do on my return trip home is to try and figure out which footprints are mine. Rarely is it obvious. Sometimes my shoe pattern gives it away. But a barefoot print is pretty indistinguishable from others walking without shoes.

Those trails of footprints also aren't straight, like they were in the picture in my parents' kitchen. They weave up and down the shore to avoid the incoming surf; take a jaunt to examine a shell, a jellyfish, or a piece of driftwood; or meander because I'm not paying attention and trying to walk in a straight line.

My realization is compared to life. Rarely do we travel in a straight line direct to a destination. We're almost never alone. Our paths intersect with others. We take excursions for the most whimsical reasons.

Sometimes the footprints disappear. I do not discount that God carries us through some of the times of our lives. But it isn't like the picture on my parents' kitchen wall. Or the poem.

Perpetuity and rhythm

We tend to define our lives by big events. Marriages and graduations. Promotions and firings. Job changes and moves. Championships and bitter losses. Maybe the ocean judges itself by things like hurricanes. But mostly it's amazing for its rhythm and regularity. Wave in. Wave out. Wave in. Wave out. Repeat, day and night, every day of the year. No breaks. No time off.

Our lives are more like waves than hurricanes. It's the daily rhythm that defines us much more than the big events.

The birds are fine

One year when we were at the beach, a flock of seagulls used our section of the beach as their gathering place. Tens of thousands of seagulls. They would arrive shortly after sunrise, seemingly appearing from nowhere and settling on the sand. It's like there was one massive invite, and everyone knew to come to that spot. Throughout the day, they would disappear, only to arrive en masse at dusk at the same location. A group meeting to watch the sunrise and sunset, every day. Sounds like a great existence to me.

"Consider the ravens, for they neither sow nor reap; they have no storeroom nor barn, and yet God feeds them; how much more valuable you are than the birds! And which of you by worrying can add a single hour to his life's span?"

Luke 12:24-25

Sharks

Though I grew up less than thirty minutes from the beach, I didn't go much as a kid, maybe only once a year. It wasn't until after high school that I even cared to spend a day with salt and sand. The summer after my high school year, I had back-to-back experiences that caused some excitement. First, I was in water that was about halfway up my chest. The lifeguard came running down the beach, blowing his whistle. He was yelling "Shark!" but I couldn't hear him. However, I saw the shark. It was swimming parallel to the shore, from right to left, about to come between me and the shore. When he (she?) got even with me, the shark turned sharply to his left and headed straight at me.

I have no idea what my heartrate was, but seeing that dorsal fin turn and come straight at me caused a significant spike in respiratory frequency. I headed for shore, knowing full well that I would be in water at least up to my hips when we met.

As the shark came closer, I could easily see the tail swishing back and forth, and eventually saw his eyes and gills. He was about six feet long. About my size, only horizontal, a whole lot sleeker, and in an environment that gave him a significant advantage. I prepared for battle. He got about six feet from me, made a sharp turn, and headed further down the beach in the direction he had started. The whole episode couldn't have lasted fifteen seconds. It felt like an hour. When I made it back to the beach, it wasn't until I sat down that I recognized my heartbeat. And my jelly legs. It took the better part of an hour for me to normalize. I didn't get in the water again that day.

The next week I did, though. Different beach. I was in water halfway up my shin. A friend, standing at the shoreline, yelled at me, "There's a shark!" and pointed right to where my feet were. I looked down and, sure enough, there was a baby brown shark, a little less than two feet long, swimming within an arm's length of my feet. He turned and was gone. I didn't swim much at the beach that summer.

The following summer I worked as an intern at the space center. One of my coworkers was going shark fishing and was super excited about the event. We got daily updates as the weekend approached. The following Monday he told his tale. The boat had travelled about 300 yards offshore and dropped anchor. He thought they would go out to sea. They could still hear people talking from the pier a little way away. They started casting and caught forty-five sharks in two hours. A few hundred yards from where people swim.

Wanna go body surfing?

Seen or not seen

People at the beach seem to fall into two broad categories.

Those that want to be seen and those that don't want to be seen. Both make me sad and curious.

There are those whose bodies are formed and shaped in a way that they think everyone wants to see. They display and show them, clearly wanting eyes on them. I suppose if I had one of those bodies and worked to keep it in that shape, I'd want people to notice and appreciate it as well. Maybe that's no different from me being a good teacher or speaker or having someone appreciate my well-groomed lawn.

There are also people whose bodies are not the picture our society portrays as sightly. And they can still want to be seen, but more for their actions than their shape. Perhaps they are loud, or drunk, or displaying feats of wonder on a board, with a kite, with a toy, or in a chair.

But sometimes it appears to go too far. They become showy, not just seen. But that means I'm applying my standards to someone else. It's what I think is proper or improper. They have their reasons; I have mine.

Then there are those that appear to want to disappear. They might have a sweatshirt and a hoodie on in the summer. They'll have sunglasses, earbuds, and a hat pulled low. They'll avoid eye contact, won't speak, and plod or jog along like they're the only person around.

If I bother to notice either group, the seen or unseen, it makes me wonder what is REALLY going on. There's a story there. A story I don't know.

Running from something

The well-worn internet joke has two friends who find

themselves in front of a charging bear. They turn and run. One man says, "We can't outrun that bear!" The other responds, "I know. I only need to outrun you."

At the beach, you see lots of joggers. I've never been a runner. I wish I could enjoy it. It's not my thing. Running on the beach is hard. Harder than running on the sidewalk. The soft sand makes it tough on the muscles. The shifting tide means you have to weave up and down the shore. You have to dodge fishermen's lines and kids' sandcastles. When you get home, there is sand in your shoes, salt in your hair, and sticky sweat all over.

But I get why you'd run on the beach. It's the same reason I walk on the beach. It's inspiring. Each step and each breath is clean and fresh.

One day as I sat like a beached whale on the shore watching whatever I could see at the coast, I saw a jogger run by. Headphones in. Lost in his own world, counting the steps or miles or time when he could get back to his house and a warm shower. I went through my little self-righteous internal monologue, wondering if he knew that walking gives 80 percent of the cardiovascular benefit of running without the bursitis. And it hit me.

You almost always see runners by themselves. Sure, there is the occasional pair but rarely a group of joggers. Most people run alone. I wonder what they're running from. People rarely run toward anything. They run from things. The runner's high, they say, is a thing to be achieved. Sounds like a drug. Something to get me out of reality. A lot like sitting idly on the beach.

Side note and parallel Deep Thought: I admire runners and

wish I had been born with the gene that liked running. And the knees and hips that could tolerate it.

Little me, big Earth

In one of his stand-up monologues, Jerry Clower relates his Uncle Versie's first trip to the beach. As he gazed upon the ocean reaching to the horizon, Uncle Versie said, "I always thought itta been bigger than this."

You can see about three miles to the horizon. Three miles in three directions. With nothing but water. The waves crashing on shore may appear to be violent, but your eyes look beyond the breakers and it appears calm. Serene. Placid. And knowing it goes on and on for a few thousand miles makes me feel small . . . .

Little Earth, big space

Now for even more perspective, walk on that beach shore at night. The sounds and smells are the same, but the sight toward the water is black. Out to sea; up in the sky. Thousands, millions, of stars. Not three miles away, but at the closest about four light years away. That's 400,000,000,000,000,000 times the distance to the horizon. The dimmest one you can see without a telescope is about 4,000 light years away, even though it is 100,000 times brighter than our sun.

Dr. Griffiths, my Introduction to Spaceflight professor, opened the semester with this statement (thirty-five years ago and I still remember it): "If you don't remember anything else from this class, remember this about space—there's a lot of it."

I'm rather confident your mind, like mine, cannot conceive

of those distances and scales. You and I are insignificant in size and mass in this universe. Thankfully, our significance isn't based on our physical mass.

You and I still matter.

Pay attention

The wonder of the beach is easily seen in children. They run at top speed toward the waves, and sometimes reverse field at top speed to get away from the same waves. They are in awe of crabs, birds, shells, formations of sand, trash, and clouds. And they want to share their wonder with anyone who will listen.

Sadly, often there is no one to listen.

I watched two small boys, probably younger than eight, arrive with their father and mother. While I could not hear them over the waves, their message was clear to both parents, "Hey! Watch this! Look at me!"

The parents were clearly on vacation. Mom was decent at giving the boys attention, even walking to the surf with them a few times. But she quickly settled in her beach chair under an umbrella with a book. A few times she mumbled when addressed without ever looking up.

Dad wasn't as attentive, and it broke my heart. It made me wonder how I acted when my children were that age. He gave his family almost no attention. He mostly fished. When his boys came up to inquire (and show him their treasures), he was short and dismissive. He didn't seem the least bit interested in his bikini-clad wife. I don't recall seeing him even speak to her. They were on the sand for several hours before packing up and returning to the house.

Vacations are nice changes from the norm with new experiences we love. I think it's worth remembering though that there aren't many things more important than our attention. And those we love know it.

Rules are for others

Posted at the public entrance to the beach:

Pets must be on leash.

Pick up after your pet.

Seen on the beach: dogs running free and lots of "residue."

Now I love a dog. Especially other people's dogs (as I have said, my favorite breed). But what is it about dog owners that makes them ignore such signs, leaving behind "presents" for others to deal with?

It's not just a phenomenon at the beach. My son and I showed up at a baseball field to practice one Sunday afternoon when he was young. Clearly posted on the fence was a sign: "No dogs on field." When we arrived, a woman was letting her pet run inside the fence. I made a comment to her, as kindly as I could, that she may have missed seeing the sign that dogs were not allowed on the field. Her response was one of exasperation and disdain. I don't recall her exact words, but the basic message was, "Who do you think I am? That rule is for the irresponsible pet owners." It included some four-letter words within earshot of my son.

I had watched her dog defecate in the outfield before we entered the field. She did nothing to clean it up. I imagined an outfielder attempting a diving catch at the next game.

My heart's desire was to know her address, have my son stomp in her dog's pile, go to her house, and wipe his cleats on her carpet. But I'm bigger than that. Some days, at least.

Why do people not adhere to rules? I drive above the posted speed limit most times when able. I cross streets at places other than crosswalks. I throw away aluminum cans (only when there isn't a recycling bin available). Why?

Because we know better. Or think we do. We like to make our own rules. (*Side note and hardly a Deep Thought: mankind has been doing that since, yes, the Garden of Eden.*)

There's always something you miss

When the kids were young, the beach was a magical place. I guess it still was when they were older; the magic just cost more. But in the toddler years, I'd ask, "What do you see?" Sometimes we'd make it a game, akin to I spy. We'd spend a few minutes spotting shells, birds, houses, people, colors, shapes, and bubbles. But there was always something else. Always something we missed at first glance. Always something one of us saw the others overlooked.

That's true of life beyond the beach. We think we have all the information. We think we see things in their entirety.

But there is always something we miss. Keep looking.

What do you think she's digging for?

We took our nephew, his wife, and their two-year-old with us to the beach. You don't need much to entertain a two-year old at the beach, but a shovel is a must.

Little Ellie took that shovel and dug and dug and dug. She was oblivious to anyone around her, the majesty of the shoreline, the sun, the gulls, or even her own hunger (that came later). She would make a hole, move, and make another. She would dig shallow trenches and draw lines in the sand.

I was sitting nearby and asked, rhetorically, "What do you think she's digging for?" The adults watching had lots of answers. They were all valid. Shells. Worms. Sharks' teeth. China. The fun of it.

On my beach walks, I watch old men (mostly) with their metal detectors and trowels trying to find Blackbeard's treasure. They methodically sweep the shore, listening for some beep in their headphones. When it makes an announcement, they kneel and dig for their treasure. I don't think I've ever seen a beachcomber shout in adulation at a discovery.

Sweet Ellie just digs. And she squeals with delight at even the slightest discovery.

I want to be like Ellie, not the old men.

16

Near-death Experiences

It wouldn't be hard to convince you that you will die. Every human meets that end. But before the final end, there are brushes with death. Some of us get closer than others, owing to factors ranging from personality to background to intelligence and chance. I've often said it's a miracle that any boy makes it to his 16th birthday.

I've had my share of close calls and scary situations. They make you think. Sometimes deeply.

Death by kite

This could easily fit in the previous chapter, but it fits here too. I was flying a stunt kite on the beach. It was a windy day. My friends were off doing their own thing, so I was sorta by myself. Getting the kite launched was an adventure. I had let the entire line play out, but that was boring. A stunt kite wasn't made to fly high and float. It can flit back and forth and do loops. I brought it back to earth where I could control it better.

As I began to test out my abilities, I realized I could make the kite fly inches off the sand and it would go really fast. But it was hard to judge how far away it was. I turned it fast and flew the other direction, with no feeling on where it was. Turned out I had let out more line than I thought and the kite went screaming right across the deck of a neighbor. The deck was full of people sunning and talking. I can't say for sure how close it came to any of them, but one man jumped in fright as the kite flew by. I'd guess it missed him by less than three feet. It was probably moving twenty miles an hour or better. And the tip was a hard plastic. Had it hit him in the face, it could easily have killed him. I was shaken with the realization. I crashed the kite on purpose into the sand and reeled it in. I was done for the weekend.

Snake

When I was a freshman in high school, my Sunday School class found out the senior boys had taken a "Survival Trip" down the St. Johns River in Florida. They only took the clothes on their back and a fishing rod for a three-day campout and river trip by canoe. Three years younger and wanting affirmation of our transition to high school, we begged our teacher to take us on a similar trip.

I can't imagine the full details of the trip ever made it to my parents. They would never have agreed to let me go had those details been known. We set out Friday evening from a launch off a local state road and headed north. We arrived at our campsite with a few hours to spare before dark. We set out fishing, because unless we caught something, we wouldn't eat that night.

The group of eight boys (and two adults) spread out along the riverbank, each hoping to be the one who landed the big catfish that would be dinner that night. I found a little spit of land that afforded me good angles to cast into the places I thought these fish were living.

After about fifteen minutes, my line snagged. I couldn't dislodge it. I went to step back to get the leverage to pull the line and break it. I don't know why, but I looked behind me as I stepped back. I was standing on a mat of woven reeds, more in the water than on the shore. As I glanced back, I saw a snake in the reeds. It's a miracle I saw him. His patterns and color were the same as the surface I was standing on. As I saw him, he saw me, and he coiled to strike. When he did that, I saw the unmistakable shape of his head and knew I was two feet from a water moccasin ready to do harm. I froze and called to my friend quietly. When I got his attention, he called our adult leader, who came walking toward me through the water. I warned him that the snake was coiled to strike and begged him not to come closer. But he kept on. When he saw the snake, he pulled out a gun (I didn't know he had one) and aimed at the snake. I asked if I should jump and run when he shot. His response: "Whatever." I didn't know he was an expert marksman. I never heard the gun go off only a few feet away. But the snake suddenly didn't have a head. Its body writhed and moved for more than a little bit. I walked up on shore and collapsed, legs shaking.

About an hour later (I had lost my appetite and was no longer fishing), we heard banging at the canoes. Our other chaperone was yelling, "Billy, come quick! I found a snake! A BIG snake!" As he jumped over canoes, the snake went under the canoes and surfaced on the other side. We could see it from shore in the early dusk. Billy arrived and shot the snake, twice. It was a VERY large moccasin, intent on doing damage.

That night we only caught two small brim and a handful of frogs (the first time in my life I ate frog legs). I found later they had found several other snakes while gigging frogs.

That night was one of the coldest of the fall season in Florida. Temps dipped near 40 degrees. The mosquitos mercilessly attacked us. I had eighty bites/welts on my hands. We huddled near the fire and tried to sleep. My shoe melted I got so close to the flames. About three a.m., two airboats arrived with the Florida Wildlife Patrol. They didn't care about our sleep and informed us of two facts. One, we were trespassing, and two, our intended campout for the second night was under four feet of water and inaccessible. The next morning we canceled the rest of our trip, pulled out at a road halfway to our destination, went out for pizza, and showed up in disgrace Sunday morning, but with stories to tell.

Canoes and low-water bridges

Maybe I should learn that canoes aren't my thing.

In graduate school, a group of six friends (including me) took a three-day canoe trip down the New River in northwestern North Carolina. I planned most of the trip (four of the six were already working full time) through phone calls, studying maps and guidebooks, and talking to the fine folks at REI. We made reservations through a guide company and headed out.

My buddy from school and I arrived early on Friday and set up camp at the outfitters. The rest arrived Friday night after dark and after the campsite was closed. We had to wake the camp host and likely woke half the camp leading our friends in. Morning arrived far too early, but we had a dawn departure scheduled.

We had packed for three days in the wilderness. We had at least six large crates, coolers, and packs, along with multiple smaller packs and gear. Each canoe had several hundred pounds of gear in it. It took more than a minute to get it all loaded, first on the bus, then on the canoes after our hour-long ride through the mountains.

As we set out, a few things became obvious. Heavy canoes ride lower. You want to travel the New River during the rainy season when the river is up. We were in the dry season. We bumped along on rocks and sandbars and frequently had to get out and wade while tugging the canoes behind us.

About an hour in, a snake slithered up beside us. I learned my canoe mate was deathly afraid of snakes. Wading was now something that wasn't as fun.

About another hour in, we came upon our first road. On the map we had, there was an inscription that said, "Portage all low-water bridges." We made comments about that but none of us knew what that meant. We didn't have to wait long to figure it out.

A low-water bridge is apparently a bridge so close to the water's surface that you can't drive a canoe under it. Our lead canoe found this out first, as the current forced them into the bridge, turned the boat sideways, tipped it over, filled it with water, and capsized it. The canoe then shot under the bridge with our two friends and all the gear from their canoe scattered in the water.

Canoe number two was close enough to shore that they were able to beach themselves before hitting the bridge.

My friend and I were lagging behind in canoe number three,

maybe 100 yards behind the others. We heard the shouting and watched the travesty unfold before us. I tried to reach for a camera when my friend said with urgency, "Hof, we're headed the same way!" And we were. We tried to reach shore, but it became obvious that we would not make it. The current swiftened, and we picked up speed, heading straight for the same fate as our friends. I don't know how we came up with the idea, but we decided to ram the piling on the bridge, which we did with significant force that nearly tossed us from the boat.

What happened next is nothing short of a miracle. The boat began to turn and as the stern caught the current, it forced the canoe forward a bit. When it had turned enough, the current also pushed against the bow. It did this right as the right side of the canoe slid down the stanchion of the bridge. The timing was almost perfect so the boat was "balanced" on the piling. The front of the boat was being hit with equal force to the back so the boat was stuck. After a few seconds to catch our breath and our wits, we climbed out of the boat onto the bridge.

There were still two very significant problems. First, our friends' boat and all of their belongings were scattered downstream and floating away. Second, our boat was still stuck on the bridge, some fifty feet from shore.

I don't recall in what order we solved those issues, but I do recall a lot of wet items being fished from the river. And I remember chaining rope and tie-down straps to guide our canoe to shore. It was a precarious mission, with the boat being dragged by the amazing force of the water. With six guys pulling, we were able to get our canoe to safety.

I wish that was the end of the story, but later that night, when we were fully exhausted, we made another navigational mistake that cost us about two hours and towing boats upstream against the mighty current to make our campsite. I saw and heard things from one of my friends that night that I'd never experienced before. We can laugh about it now, but it was a harrowing experience and a trip I will never forget.

Some lessons learned:

- Water is powerful. A human is no match for its force.
- Planning is important. Know what you're getting into.
- It's good to know when someone is past their limit. That's not a time for jokes.
- Carry your own gear. That way if it gets messed up, you can accept the consequences of your own actions and not lay blame on someone else.

Ocean raft

For many years, my in-laws took an annual trip to the coast for a week each summer. It included multiple families, lots of kids, ridiculous amounts of food, and plenty of mayhem. But most of the family had different joys than me. I like to be on the sand at the beach, not inside or on the porch. Most of the adults on our trips didn't want to venture too far from the house. But the kids (nieces and nephews) did.

One day of particularly rough seas, we listened to the pleas of the children to go to the water. I was the only adult willing to get in. We had a rubber raft to play around with in the water. Somehow, I ended up in the raft, with my nephew—probably about ten years old—tugging on the rope trying to keep me from floating away.

A large wave came up, bigger than either of us. As it started to lift the boat, he held on both for his own balance and also as my escort. The wave hit the boat sideways and threw me into the air.

I don't recall thinking anything other than, "I am not in control here." I did a full flip and landed awkwardly on my feet in a squatting position. I first thought I had blown out my knee. But I didn't have long to think, as another wave smashed me down and knocked me onto the shore. I lay there for what seemed like minutes, trying to get a bead on my condition. I hurt, but wasn't even sure where. I limped ashore, went inside, got clean, and laid down to sleep. In a few days I was fine. I'm not sure if there was another adult chaperone on the beach. Nobody died.

The thought that haunts me to this day is that I could have just as easily landed on my head as my feet. I could easily be a paraplegic from that event. Only the whim of gravity or the grace of God let me land the way I did. Years later a friend broke his neck. His surgeon said there were four things he wouldn't do or let his kids do: dive into water they couldn't see through, ride a horse, ride a motorcycle, and body surf at the beach. I see why.

Years later, my nephew asked me if I remembered that event. He admitted it still gave him chills to think about. He isn't alone.

The first time driving

When I got my driver's permit at age fifteen, Mom took me to the church parking lot to practice. We did left and right turns, panic stops, and tried parking. Then she said, "Why don't you drive home?" It had never crossed my mind that I would drive home.

The car was a 1969 Chevrolet Kingswood Estates station wagon. It was perhaps the largest consumer automobile ever created. The road home was a very narrow road with no shoulder. There was not any room for error.

After being told that there was no other option other than me driving us home (which now seems so out of character for my mom), I set out. About a quarter mile into our journey on narrow Park Avenue, I looked up and saw a semi-truck coming toward us. The road seemed incredibly narrow. Mom simply said, "Keep it on your side of the road." I lined up best I knew how and did something they never discussed in the driver's handbook: I closed my eyes. A few seconds (probably milliseconds) later, I opened them to find the truck only visible in the rear view mirror and my car still on the road. I've never been frightened of narrow roads since.

The first time driving a bus

That bus driving job I had may have been the favorite employment of my life. Every week a new destination, a new group, a new experience. All on someone else's dime.

But it didn't begin well. I took a trial trip with the company to see whether I would like it. Even though I had a commercial bus driver's license, I was told I wouldn't drive, only work with the team to provide services and work with the passengers to entertain. I liked that plan.

On our last night, as we headed home, we pulled off at a rest stop to let the driver have some relief. He told me, "It's your turn to drive." I protested. I've never driven. I'm tired. There are people who need to live. He promised to stay up and supervise. I don't know why he let (forced) me to drive or why I agreed to, but when the bus pulled out of that rest stop sometime after midnight, I was behind the wheel.

I eased through the parking lot with him guiding me through every turn. I merged onto I-75 south out of Chattanooga to join the truckers for the night haul. About ten minutes later, my supervisor yawned and said I was doing great, he was going to sleep. I was the only one awake with 47 sleepers in the back of my bus.

About ten minutes later, I-75 took a massive sharp turn. It had to be non-standard for an interstate. I noted there was a semi-truck directly beside me. I don't have any idea how I kept the bus in my lane and on the highway. Upon exiting the turn I saw a precipice on the other side of the guardrail. Had I slipped, we would have gone to a certain death.

A few hours later, I was driving through downtown Atlanta on a Sunday morning. That's the best time to go through Atlanta, but it was still busy. We ended that leg at Stone Mountain State Park. Somehow I got the bus parked. I was exhausted.

Thankfully, bus drivers are vetted a little better these days than when I started. But there has to be a first time you do anything. Excuses aren't worth anything.

Wrong exit

My first summer out of college, I moved back home and didn't have a full-time job (or a career, but that's a story for another place in Deep Thoughts). That caused a lot of tension with the people who were paying my rent (the 'rents), so I got a job driving buses for a charter company. We primarily worked with churches and youth, taking them on long trips that were normally inaccessible to them. My first trip was taking a youth group from Lakeland, FL, to a conference in Buffalo, NY. That's a long way to drive.

This group decided to take advantage of the long trip and see the sights up the east coast of the United States. We spent a day in Washington, DC, a night and a day at Gettysburg, a day in Philadelphia, and a day in New York City. As one of the drivers, I got to do everything they did, except I got paid for all that fun.

As we were transiting Philadelphia, we ran into a good bit of road construction. Apparently in the northeast, they do all their road maintenance in the summer. They had whole exits shut down, multiple lanes of road closed, and massive detours. For a little context, this was 1990. There was no GPS. No cell phones. Our trips were planned from the corporate office with an Atlas, with driving directions printed out for us days in advance. Any deviations made that planning obsolete. We did have CB radios to communicate between the buses.

One of the buses was running low on fuel and we had mapped out an exit for a stop. When we got to that exit, it was closed. We jumped on the CB and decided to take the next exit and circle back. Except the next exit didn't have an on ramp back on the highway, so we ended up on a thoroughfare parallel to the interstate. With no way to turn around, we began to drive into a … less ritzy section of town. It became obvious we were headed for "the Hood." The lead driver radioed that he was going to turn off onto a side road to turn around. He turned right at the next intersection. As soon as we turned in we knew it was a mistake. The road narrowed quickly. We saw a sign that said "No Exit." There were people everywhere. Kids in the street. Men sitting on crates on porches. We were pretty confident there were multiple drug deals going on in sight of the 90-plus kids we were toting around. Everyone stopped what they were doing to watch these two buses slowly inch their way down the street.

"What do we do?" crackled over the CB. "We'll have to back up." There was no other option. Except we were now blocking traffic, and the only way to turn around a 40-foot bus would mean getting it backed into a six-lane road. There would have to be people on the outside of the bus helping us. No one in the street seemed to want to assist.

Our driver who wasn't behind the wheel volunteered to jump out and help us. We joked that we weren't stopping to pick up his body, but that seemed like a legitimate possibility. He jumped out and tried to ask in a friendly way if we could turn around. Several men shook their head without getting off their crates. Finally, a younger (maybe mid twenties) man and his friend sauntered over to strike up conversation. I don't know what our driver said or did, but they walked down the street with us backing up (beeping noises attracting more attention) and into that six-lane road to give us the space to turn around. The whole episode lasted maybe three minutes. But it felt like an hour. When done, our driver boarded again and confessed he had never been so scared in his life. He said he gave the guys $10 each on his way back to the bus.

Some Deep Thoughts upon reflecting on that incident.

- When the plan isn't working, sticking to the plan isn't a great idea.

- The first exit is often not the right exit.
- Don't be afraid to ask for help, even from people who may not look like they want to help.

First-time pilots

When I went to a pilot training center to fly a full-motion 737 simulator, they told me that jet planes were too expensive to fly for pilot training. The first time a pilot ever flies a new type of passenger plane is with paying passengers in the back. Comforting.

Flying

For about ten years during my first midlife crisis, my primary passion and hobby was aviation. I got my private pilot certificate, my instrument rating, and my commercial license. I even bought a plane.

The public sees flying as inherently dangerous. I would choose the word "unforgiving." Per mile traveled, it's no more dangerous than a car. And unlike driving, almost all the mishaps are a result of pilot error. I was the most significant factor in my flying safety. But, unlike a car, you can't coast to a stop or pull off at the first sign of trouble.

But with two small kids and a flying-averse spouse, I lived with the constant pressure to make sure I didn't make a dumb mistake to become a bad pilot statistic. When I stopped flying for financial reasons, I had accrued about 500 hours of varied flight time and a nice collection of adventures. I was reminiscing with a pilot friend recently about how close we had ever come to mishap. Like car drivers, there are always near misses.

I had two close encounters with other aircraft. One, a helicopter in the wrong place and altitude near an airport, was on my first or second solo flight. It scared me enough I landed and waited a bit to calm down. Another was two planes in open space, and it's a good thing there's a lot of space. Once I pushed a banked turn a little hard and lost more altitude than I should have, but I started the turn at 3,000 feet and never came close to disaster. The same turn in a traffic pattern would not have had a good ending. And I pressed through a small layer of reported ice to get to clear air on top. Turns out there was no ice on my route, but those two minutes in the clouds were nerve-wracking.

I miss flying. But as I age, I am clearly not as sharp as I once was. I can get good again. But if I can't get (really) good, I won't do it, because as a pilot, I'm the single greatest factor in my safety.

Fireworks

For years, a group of four families vacationed together for the Fourth of July. The kids were young, under ten. One year we had a few firecrackers. The next, we added bottle rockets. Then mortars. And more mortars. A potato cannon. Eventually we had a pretty nice show of loud noises and flashing lights.

One year, one of our troupe had the idea as we were shooting off the fireworks to tie two of the mortars together for twice the show. We twisted the two fuses together and lit them. The first two shots went off simultaneously. What a show! The next one alerted us that things had gone awry. One shot at about a 45-degree angle sideways, and the next went horizontal in the opposite direction. We ran and dove for cover, which is rather sparse in an open field. The mortars appeared to be spinning, shooting explosions in every direction. To our horror, the next one shot toward the house, maybe seventy-five yards away. Our wives and children were sitting on the porch. We watched the trail of the firework hit one of the tents in the field. I expected the tent (mine) to erupt in flames. Instead, we saw (and heard) a large explosion at ground level about fifty yards on the other side of the tent. The projectile had gone straight through the nylon of the tent.

I'm guessing there were close to a dozen mortars in all. Fortunately, no others went off in the direction of the house.

Thinking about that night gives me chills to this day. Had the projectile gone five degrees to the left, the mortar would have exploded on the porch, likely killing most of our families. Had it gone five degrees to the right, it would have torched one (or more) of our vehicles. It could easily have gone through one of us and not the tent. But it didn't.

The "great idea" caused the fuse to burn a hole in the side of the mortar tube, exploding one in place and knocking the whole assembly over. As the next mortar would shoot, the force of its launch would cause the mortar tube to spin. Had they not been tied together, they might have even been shooting from other than ground level.

God was gracious that night. What could have been is not something I like to dwell on. I deserved worse than a harrowing story to add to a book.

We didn't scuttle the fireworks shows (which in retrospect would have been the prudent decision). But we did implement a safety shield and "safe house" plan that wouldn't allow a projectile to head toward the house. And we never tied fuses together again.

Potato cannon

About that potato cannon. That thing was pretty amazing (if I do say so myself: I designed and built it). With a set of interchangeable PVC barrels, it would shoot golf balls (300+ yards), potatoes (mostly obliterated), and tennis balls. We could get eleven seconds of hang time from a tennis ball. Physics will tell us that means it was reaching a height of almost 500 feet and was leaving the barrel at 120 miles per hour.

After oohing and aahing, we decided it would be a great idea and even better practice to send the young boys out to shag flies shot out of this contraption. Except it shot the balls so high they couldn't see them. On about try three, my son saw the ball at the last second and tried to move to catch it. Except the ball came down at about the same speed (less a little air resistance) it went up. His reaction wasn't fast enough, and the ball hit him square in the eye. He dropped like a sack of potatoes, idiom/pun intended.

As he sat screaming in agony, the only thought I had was that I had blinded my son doing something stupid. We iced his eye and calmed him down. He was a tough cookie—still is. He had a black eye, but no damage. But it could have been …

Boys (of all ages) don't usually think of consequences when adventure is afoot. It's always worth stopping to ask, "What's the worst thing that could happen?" and have a voice of reason think that through before doing things involving high velocity and force.

17

Questions (Without Answers)

As a teacher at heart, I love to ask questions. Like Socrates.[20] But not all questions have answers. Or at least not good ones.

Low-dollar theft

I was in need of a special metric nut for a home project. The metric nuts are rare and housed in a drawer in the fasteners aisle at your local home improvement store. They are indexed with pictures and are rather easy to find. Except there were almost never any nuts in the bin. I went to three different stores and found the same story at each place. The bin containing M6x1.0 nylon lock nuts always had the packaging, but the packages were torn open and the nuts were gone. I'm guessing people needed one nut and didn't want to buy a package with two nuts in it. So they took one nut. Then someone else lifted the remaining nut.

20 https://en.wikipedia.org/wiki/Socratic_method

Why would someone steal the contents of a $1.25 package of metric nuts? Those of us willing to pay the price can't even obtain the product because the store never knew their inventory was low. I don't understand the mindset of low-dollar theft.

High-dollar theft

I do understand high dollar theft. It's credit without having to pay it back. Assuming you aren't caught. But like materialism, it's a dangerous game. It cannot be satisfied. And it is . . . illegal. With high consequences.

And while I understand it, I don't condone or participate in it. Doing so says a lot about the character of the one who thinks that's the way to get ahead.

The most likely thing

One of the questions I ask in my strategic thinking seminar is "What's the most likely outcome?" Most of us possess enough experience and imagination to be able to predict what will happen in many areas of our lives. Sure, rare, random outcomes do occur. But for the most part, we know the results of our actions. And we can order our world and our decisions on the probability of those outcomes. Insurance companies make a lot of money doing this. It's called risk management.

It's also a great antidote for worry.

What will happen? We cannot know.

What will likely happen? The answer usually tells us our direction.

Mad, sad, and glad

Got this from a book. Or maybe a podcast. It's questions to ask family members at the end of the day:

- Who made you mad?
- Who made you sad?
- What made you glad?

Good questions.

Worry

My grandmother was a worrier. Once while sitting on the front porch, she said, "I feel like I should be worrying about something, but I don't know what it is." Her children joked that none of them had to worry about anything because Mama did enough for all of them.

Crazy thing about worry is that it doesn't affect anything except your own health. And not for the better. Yet still we persist. It's not logical. It doesn't make sense. We worry anyway.

"And which of you by worrying
can add a single hour to his life's span?"

Luke 12:25

There's a good question in that scripture. And the answer is: nobody. Grandmama lived to be ninety-eight, mostly healthy until the end. Imagine the length of her life if she hadn't been such a worrier!

18

So What?

I've got more thoughts. Some of them may one day be Deep Thoughts. Some thoughts have changed in the process of writing this book. Deep thinking isn't an action you finish, and Deep Thoughts are not set in stone.

You may not think any of my thoughts are particularly deep. I'm okay with that. You can have your own Deep Thoughts about these or other topics.

Let's circle back. Deep Thoughts have three components and each requests an action from you:

1. Deep Thoughts are a subset of thoughts.
   Think more.

2. Deep Thoughts need to be remembered.
   Write them down.

3. Deep Thoughts need to be shared.
   Start today.

That's it. If you've read anything in this book that made you think, consider how you could do the same for someone else.

Practically, consider when and where you are at your best. Pick the time of day when you won't be interrupted. Pick a place or setting that makes you smile. Put the phone on mute, or better yet, leave it behind. Be quiet. Listen. Think. Do it regularly.

Start a journal. It will be a blessing to you and those you share it with. There's no right way or wrong way or good way or bad way to collect your thoughts and organize them. Do what works for you. But do it.

The last action may be the most important. Share what you're thinking. For many, this may be an obstacle. You don't want to share half-thought ideas or your personality prefers to form your thoughts before you speak. I get it. I'm married to one of those. But your friends and family and the rest of the world probably don't care. Just share.

You may need to muster some courage. Many (most?) of our relationships are so shallow that asking deep questions may not go over well at first. Dig deep. Instead of asking if they've seen the latest Netflix episode, ask them what they think about . . . whatever.

Find some cards or games that encourage conversation. I've used the Chat Pack sets of "Fun Questions to Spark Entertaining Conversations" (available on Amazon). I also have a set of high-quality picture cards with prompts on them that I use. They were originally designed for an eldercare facility to help their residents tell their stories. They work great for the not-so-elderly as well.

Here are some of my favorite dinner party questions:

- What would you do if you had nothing to do?
- What would you do if you found $1? $10? $100? $1,000. $10,000, $100,000, $1,000,000, $10,000,000? How about $100,000,000? (no tax implications and no accountability)
- Why do you think most lottery winners end up miserable?
- If all jobs paid the same, what would you do?
- If you could have dinner with anyone in all of history, who would it be and what would you ask them?
- What are the activities on your bucket list (the things you want to do before you die)?
- What is a skill or talent you wish you had, but don't possess (yet)?
- When were you the happiest?

And here are some conversation starters I use in my public speaking classes:

- What was your first job?
- What was the first car you bought?
- What is a product that you love?
- What is a cause that you support?

- What is a place you want to visit?
- What is a treasured gift you have received?
- Who is your favorite relative?

Stories and conversations spark thought. While I was writing this, I had a call from a friend, which is unusual. Mostly I get texts from him. He'd been reading a book that made him have some insights that connected with some conversations we had. He called to tell me that he felt I was on the right track and to thank me for pushing our conversations and friendship above and beyond the superficial. It was an encouragement to me. But I only received that because he shared. And he only responded because I shared.

The world would be a better place if we all shared our thinking more.

Let it begin with you.

About the Author

Alan Hoffler grew up around America's Space Program, the son of a NASA doctor for the Apollo astronauts. The youngest of three children, he was fortunate enough to be raised in an environment where he could learn a lot about a lot. His varied interests have led him on a wild career chase that included driving tour buses, teaching public high school and college math, testing computer software, training in the corporate world, giving lectures nationally on pilot safety, and starting several businesses. For the last twenty years, his primary vocation has been as a public speaking coach, helping others to craft and deliver their message to the world. His underlying life purpose is to free people from the trap of mediocrity and open them to embrace excellence in what they do.

Along the way, he's pursued aviation/flying, sports and coaching, vegetable gardening, woodworking, stained glass, disc golf, laser engraving, and pickleball. He loves sunsets over bodies of water.

His first published writing, "Essay on an Essay," won third place in a county-wide contest in the fifth grade. He has gone on to author *Presentation Sin*, and co-author *6 Steps*

Forward and *Silver Goldfish*. His latest project is a video training program for aspiring speakers called Online Stage Coach (www.onlinestagecoach.com).

He has two titanium hips and a bum knee but chases life with full abandon and a zest that wants to be at full throttle when the end finally comes. He and his wife Haley reside in Apex, North Carolina, and are the proud parents of three amazing young adults: two born into the family and a third who married in.

If you have suggestions or comments about his writings, would like to schedule a workshop or speaking event, or need to share your Deep Thoughts with someone, you can contact him at:

alan@alanhoffler.com

You also can download a free discussion guide with deep questions for you to ponder at:

www.alanhoffler.com/deepthoughts

Future Books by Alan Hoffler

Stan Phelps, my co-author for Book #3, Silver Goldfish, gives this advice to aspiring authors. It's his sure-fire method[21] for getting a book published.

1. Select a title
2. Design the cover[22]
3. Set a publication date
4. Tell everyone about your book, show them the cover, and tell them the date.

It must work. He's written a dozen books, and as far as I know, they've all been released on time.

I'm not quite as prolific or disciplined as Stan, but I'm willing to tell the world what I'm working on. I have thirty or so books I wish to complete before I depart the planet.

Started but not completed

- ***Wyck*** — My dad is an amazing man with a wild story. I'd like to help him tell it, through his memoirs. I better hurry. He's 90. We discovered Storii[23] and Dad is recording two nuggets every night to help in the project.
- ***Intermission*** — Taken from the metaphor of hockey, this would be a look at the importance of taking breaks in our lives.

---

21 https://www.youtube.com/watch?v=VxOJ48DWzak
22 https://boxshot.com/3d-book-cover/
23 www.storii.com

- ***The Simple-Hard: Why putting in the time gets you what you want*** — This is a classic consultant's quadrant examining the implications of mastering the difficult and easy when overlayed with complex and simple tasks.
- ***The Big Buts of the Bible (with Dr. Gary Moger)*** — One of the most powerful words of the Bible is the word "but." It changes everything.
- ***The Scalpel of the Great Physician*** — Having had four major surgeries, I've learned a lot about physical suffering and the road back to wholeness. I believe it's a perfect metaphor for how our lives and relationships can be restored.
- ***The Virtual Speaker*** — I've got a video series about how to deliver content online, but I'd like to write a finish to my book about it as well.

Only an idea and an outline:

- ***Reared Weird*** — a catalog of traits my siblings and I noticed that made our parents different; most of them were noble and good for us
- ***The Date / The Bucket List for Dads*** — a look at what every dad should do before his children leave home
- ***Tell Your Story*** — a book on why and how to tell your story effectively
- ***Rec Sports Coaches' Handbook*** — a guide for recreation coaches on how to impact young lives through the second tier of competitive sports based on what I've learned partnering with 3D Institute on how to coach effectively

- ***Chasing Sunsets*** — why everyone needs something beautiful to pursue
- ***The Four Questions (#1)*** — taken from the definition of my favorite word ("Coach"), a deep-dive into the four questions that definition raises
- ***The Four Questions (#2)*** — taken from Joe Ehrmann's InsideOut Coaching book, the four questions that can change your life
- ***Ten Meter Champion*** — the most important metrics to track in life and what their results tell us
- ***Call Me Coach*** — why I resonate with the greatest title ever and why taking the identity of coach gives a life purpose and direction
- ***Things You Don't Have to Teach Boys (and Things You Do/Should)*** — a treatise on learning manhood
- ***Becoming the Man I've Always Dreamed Of Being*** — how to bridge the gap between hopes/ dreams and reality
- ***You Can't Lose What You Don't Have*** — why getting attention is the lost secret to "impact"
- ***Uncommon Sense (with Eric Hoffler?)*** — a collection of aphorisms and truths
- ***The Questions of God*** — a look at questions God/ Jesus asks throughout the Bible—and truths to be learned from them
- ***Conditional Love*** — taking a look at the statements promised to us in the Bible that begin with the word "IF"—a combination of philosophy and math

- ***Parable of Moses*** — a retelling of this compelling story in the context of the 21st century (It'd make a good movie too.)
- ***Practical Proverbs*** — a catalog of the truths in Proverbs by topic
- ***Prone to Excess*** — thoughts on why we are so compelled to addictions, good and bad (I need a partner who is an expert in human behavior for this one.)
- ***The Art of the Shut Up*** — the power of the pause
- ***Behind the Speaker*** — a look into what happens before, during, and after a speaker gets on stage to deliver an amazing talk; a look into the preparation, mind, and circumstances that lead to greatness
- ***Nine Lives*** — a science fiction book where each member of a group is granted nine lives with the ultimate point to answer the question, "What would you die for?"
- ***Confessions of an Old Young Man*** — a look at the mindset on aging, since no one feels old
- ***Runway 89: The Numbers of Aviation*** — catalog the myriad of rules and numbers to make it easier for aspiring pilots to learn the rules of the air (One of the greatest barriers to getting a pilot's license is learning all the rules of the air.)

And, of course,

- ***More Deep Thoughts from the Shallow End***

Made in the USA
Columbia, SC
03 July 2025

60265337R00122